For –

Terri,

dear niece –
sweet, kind person.
– a little glimpse
into your past.

Love,
Aunty Pavé.
x

Objects in Mirror Are Closer than They Appear

A Memoir

Pauline A.G. Johansen

iUniverse, Inc.
Bloomington

Copyright © 2010 by Pauline A.G. Johansen

All rights reserved. No part of this book may be used or reproduced by any means, graphic, electronic, or mechanical, including photocopying, recording, taping or by any information storage retrieval system without the written permission of the publisher except in the case of brief quotations embodied in critical articles and reviews.

The views expressed in this work are solely those of the author and do not necessarily reflect the views of the publisher, and the publisher hereby disclaims any responsibility for them.

iUniverse books may be ordered through booksellers or by contacting:

iUniverse
1663 Liberty Drive
Bloomington, IN 47403
www.iuniverse.com
1-800-Authors (1-800-288-4677)

Because of the dynamic nature of the Internet, any Web addresses or links contained in this book may have changed since publication and may no longer be valid. The views expressed in this work are solely those of the author and do not necessarily reflect the views of the publisher, and the publisher hereby disclaims any responsibility for them.

Any people depicted in stock imagery provided by Thinkstock are models, and such images are being used for illustrative purposes only.

Certain stock imagery © Thinkstock.

ISBN: 978-1-4502-7305-3 (sc)
ISBN: 978-1-4502-7307-7 (hc)
ISBN: 978-1-4502-7306-0 (ebook)

Printed in the United States of America

iUniverse rev. date: 2/14/2011

With love to
my Family

I didn't remember it all...
but I remember the love.

And
Arne and Samantha
You know why.

Table of Contents

Chapter One	Getting to Know the Virgin	1
Chapter Two	What Have You Done For Me Lately?	10
Chapter Three	But Can You Clean?	26
Chapter Four	Jack-of-All-Trades	33
Chapter Five	Once Upon A Time	41
Chapter Six	You Are What You Eat	57
Chapter Seven	What Doesn't Kill You	64
Chapter Eight	Poor Is A Four Letter Word	69
Chapter Nine	This Way Home	74
Chapter Ten	Just Like Everyone Else	87
Chapter Eleven	Driving Crazy	93
Chapter Twelve	Surprise!	97
Chapter Thirteen	Gone Cruisin'	105
Chapter Fourteen	It's A Long Way To Tipperary	124

Anita, Peter, Dad (with John), Eileen, Mom (with Tony), Helena, Pauline

Getting to Know the Virgin

Our Lady of Sorrows lived in an alcove on the second floor of my elementary school. Taller than any woman I knew, she wore a long blue gown over a white shift and held baby Jesus in her stiff, unmotherly arms. Her gold-crowned head was slightly tilted, looking down in abject acceptance of her lot. Her tight-lipped smile spoke of all the pain she had suffered. Standing there greeting us every day, her unspoken message was, "You did this; you broke my heart." And everything we heard and were taught every day reminded us we were dirty, filthy little sinners who broke Mary's heart and we could never make it better. But we damn well better try.

Sometimes I used to just stand and stare up at her in her tiny home and wonder what happened at night. Did she put down that chubby old man/baby, stretch her arms high above her head, sit down on the edge of her alcove, dangle her legs back and forth, sigh and wish for a different fate? Did she wish herself away from there? I did, every day—to anywhere else.

I began biting my nails shortly after starting school. I bit hard and often, and none of the usual remedies helped. My mom tried pepper, disgusting clear liquids "guaranteed to stop the urge," socks tied on my hands and the usual round of threats. There were no bribes; our family didn't believe in bribes. I was made of strong stuff, though, and I bit anyway until they bled. I bit the nail and the skin around the nail, and I continued to bite even when there was nothing left to bite.

I had a reason to bite. I had to go to school. This instilled stomach-churning, cramping fear, because I knew that what lay ahead would make me feel stupid and worthless and that there would be no way out.

Home, on the other hand, was loud and confusing and a constant swirl of busyness. Before my school days, I often hid behind a couch or in a cupboard. Even though I was only five, Mom would find me something to do, like holding the bottle in the baby-of-the-moment's mouth, or drying the dishes. But I wanted to talk and sing all day. I danced around in my socks and spun around on the linoleum floor on my bum in my flannel pyjamas. Mostly I sat and did nothing. I got hugged, and yelled at. I got fed and I slept. I didn't know it, but that was as good as it was going to get, because then school began. I was not prepared for what today we might call the lifestyle change.

I started Grade 1 when I was five, but I was more like a three-year-old. In addition to biting my nails I still sucked the two fingers on my right hand at night. I had thick, raised calluses there. The sound drove my sister Anita crazy. I never heard myself, but she told me it was a bit like wet nails on a blackboard. Poor Anita; because she was closest to me in age she always got to sleep with me. My eldest sister, Helena, and Eileen, the youngest girl for the moment, at least slept together. They listened to Anita's complaints with smug smiles.

The anxiety began the moment I woke up and realized I had another school day ahead of me. When you're five years old, one day seems forever, a school year an unimaginable length of time stretching ahead farther than you can see. Like thinking about infinity, it gave me a terrible headache. The one or two moments of grace before I got up in the morning were squandered on a prayer to have a truck run over my thumb. This would be painful, yes—debilitating, even—but not life-threatening. It would guarantee I could stay home.

I pictured my thumb hugely bandaged, throbbing; the pity I would receive and the soup and tea in bed. It would be a terrific way to avoid the yelling, humiliation and fear that came with school. Getting your thumb run over made a lot more sense than, say, your toe. Sure, you would get some sympathy for that, but let's face it: they would still send you to school and you would still be expected to do your work. There would still be the big, fat pencil, the paper so thin it ripped the first time you erased, creating a big hole. No, it had to be the thumb. No other body part would do.

If I was scared I couldn't control my bladder. Most of the time I just wanted to have a nap. But it was true I could read and my mother had other babies around, and so I went to school. Beyond being able to read I had absolutely no school-ready skills. I had no idea how to hold a pencil, use a pair of scissors or any notion at all about what a number was or what you did with it.

Then came Our Lady of Sorrows Parents' Open House. The idea was for parents to accept the nuns' invitation to drop in any time during the day and witness the stellar learning experiences their children were having. For many parents it was probably also a chance to see their kid shine at something. The plan was that when a parent knocked on the door, someone would jump up and invite them in. Then the lesson that was being taught would be used as an excuse to call on the parent's child.

Mom knocked. We were doing math.

"Welcome, Mrs. Go-jev-ik. Pauline, stand up and count backwards from forty-nine," she said sweetly.

I was confused. She didn't talk like that. I stalled. I looked around the room. I opened my eyes wide.

"Me? You mean me?"

I gave a look that was meant to signal surprise and great, good humour. Then I glanced over my shoulder and all around the room, pretending there was another Pauline in the room and another Mrs. Gojević. I was hoping she would get frustrated or bored and call on someone else. Right.

"Stand up, Pauline. Count backwards from forty-nine," she repeated just a bit more loudly and a bit more in the voice I recognized. I stood up.

What's a forty-nine? We could have been talking quantum physics. I launched into a stream of numbers I did know.

"Uh, seventy-seven, twenty-nine, thirty-one?"

I tried as many numbers as I could, hoping I might just hit on it by accident. I didn't, but she wasn't going to let me off.

"Come on, dear. I know you can try harder than that," she commanded.

"Dear?" Is she talking to me? And, no, I couldn't try harder. The effort was already making me want to throw up.

So I continued. "Fifty, forty-six, eleven?"

I didn't look at the nun or my mom. I stared hard at the floor, hoping for inspiration. My mom put an end to the agony.

"Oh, that's all right, Sister. She can count with me when she gets home."

I looked up at her. She looked like an angel. But she was certainly not a happy one.

"But really, Mrs. Go-je-vik, we should insist; this is very important," the nun said with barely controlled fury.

"Well, we will get to it, I assure you," Mom said in her very best plummy British accent.

She looked so beautiful that day. She had her hat and gloves on, and her red lipstick—the only piece of makeup she owned was perfectly applied. I felt so proud of her, and so ashamed of myself. And then my mother left.

She never mentioned it that night, but I am sure she was thinking, *"Well, there goes the cosy retirement."*

Obviously, I didn't shine at school, and, next to my eldest brother, Peter, I had the worst reputation for misbehaving. The nun who taught Grade 1 was a caricature of an angry, bitter person. How could anyone always be so frustrated and disappointed? You would think that at least once during the day she would find a moment of happiness and it would be reflected in her eyes, and maybe even in the way she treated a bunch of little kids.

Her face was tanned, and I think she may have been of Mediterranean ancestry. She looked like an evil Mother Theresa and was in fact capable of inflicting harm. She seemed to resent us, and she liked to show it in hands-on ways. I have a memory of her grabbing my ear and pulling at it until it bled. I'm sure I deserved it—no doubt for some transgression like laughing or talking, both of which were forbidden and both of which I could not stop doing.

Objects in Mirror Are Closer than They Appear

There were fifty of us in that classroom—fifty crying, pant-wetting, totally uninterested noisy kids. To deal with us she devised a scheme worthy of any Third World tin-pot dictator. It worked like this: if you transgressed during the week your name would go up on a board. For every misdemeanour a tick went next to your name. Often only my name and one other child's would be up there. The week went on, the ticks grew. Friday was reckoning day, when you went into the cloakroom at the back of the class and received hits from a long wooden ruler on your hand equal to the number of ticks. It was the perfect punishment, combining day-to-day worry and fear with the culminating beating. I spent a lot of time in that cloakroom. Today, if I catch a whiff of a certain smell that hung over that space—a mingling of musty coats, rotten banana, dust and old cardboard boxes—I am back there with feelings of the same fear and loathing.

Sometimes I managed to convince my mother I was sick on a Friday. This was a real sacrifice on my part; that usually meant she would keep me in bed on Saturday too. It was a tough decision, but the thought of another beating was enough incentive to tolerate a day in my room.

I was clearly a kid in distress. In addition to biting and sucking my fingers, I ate things I shouldn't. At home I ate dirt—not big handfuls of it; it was more dirt that was stuck to other things. At least my mother said I ate dirt. Otherwise, why did I have worms?

"Have you been eating dirt again?" she would ask, watching me absentmindedly scratching at my bum, a telltale sign. Of course I denied it vehemently; I knew the cure.

The usual remedy for worms was to drink something really nasty, which apparently scared the worms and sent them running out your bum like cowards. Then you had to lie over your mother's knee while she pried open your cheeks to look for escapees. Sometimes she showed them to me. They were little and white and wiggly.

I'm surprised that anything still embarrasses me. You would think that having someone root out worms from your bum would make everything else seem like a mere nothing. But I guess, like your nose, which keeps growing until you die, you just never lose the ability to feel the burn of shame. Indeed, I kept embarrassment and shame close at hand as a kid through a series of small and large ridiculous behaviours, either on my part or on the part of others.

There was, for example, that little matter of my eating in school. I ate mostly erasers, paper and glue. I ate a really incredible amount of glue. With that lovely peppermint smell that glue was almost like food. The erasers had a smell, too: a soft, pinky smell just a little bit like strawberry ice cream. In the case of erasers it was more the texture I was after. You could chew and chew and chew one eraser all afternoon. You could break off small pieces and stick them between your teeth and then dig them out and chew. All of this was time-consuming and required commitment to the task. While I was busy chowing down on a Pink Pearl or a sheet of lined foolscap, I wasn't thinking about anything. I was lost in the moment of smell and taste and swallow. I needed those moments of escape.

It could, however, be difficult when you were loaned an eraser and you ate it and the loaner wanted it back. I'd lie and say I gave it to someone else. That "someone" would, of course, deny it, and I'd just shrug. *What could you do? Some people were such liars.*

So there we were, all of us in the Grade 1 classroom on the first floor of Our Lady of Sorrows School. The desks were nailed to runners, five rows of ten seats. One behind the other we sat and sat and sat.

We sat while she called out names of students to read at random from the Dick and Jane reader. Most often these round-robin reading sessions left me so bored I wanted to claw my eyes out. There was always some poor kid stumbling over "Run, Spot, Run." I wanted to shout at them, "Are you stupid? It says 'Run,' not 'Bun.' Bun, Spot, Bun? Idiots."

It did no good to shoot looks of anger and derision their way; nobody cared, and the readers were immersed in their own private hell. But I was so angry at the wicked waste of my talent. Here was the only thing I was good at and it was turned into torture.

There were moments of glorious release from the grind of school. The rare occasions when we stood beside our desks, swaying every so slightly back and forth while keeping our legs stationary, and sang, "Here we go loop de loo, here we go loop de lie." Those brief moments were transcendental for me. I lost myself as I swayed and sang and sang, a big goofy smile on my face just as if this were a normal school and I were a normal kid.

Most of the time was spent filling in workbook pages or copying lines and lines of nonsense from the blackboard. I sat and endlessly filled in those workbooks with my poorly formed letters. All that sitting can do strange things to a five-year-old, particularly as my bowels were even more unreliable than my bladder, especially when we were doing things that made me nervous—which meant anything but reading. Leaving the room was not allowed, however.

We would be doing math and my gut would be sympathetically churning. I'd ask to go, and then ask to go again, and Sister would repeat through gritted teeth, "You are not leaving this room until I let you, you lazy, lazy girl. You finish your work. You will regret it if you ask me again."

She wasn't completely correct. It was true I didn't want to do the math, but I would have if I'd thought there was a glimmer of a hope I would get any of it right. I knew I wouldn't. I never did. And I knew she meant it when she said not to ask again, so I did the only thing I could do. I did it in my underpants and had to sit on it for the rest of the afternoon. The effect was to create a very dry poo sandwich that stuck both to my bum and my panties. I sat very, very still. It was probably the stillest I have ever been in my life. When it was time to go I waddled home beside my sister Anita.

"Why are you walking like that?"

"I pooped my pants."

Anita, who usually protected me, was clearly in no mood to make me feel better.

"You are in so much trouble."

She was probably worried that somehow she would be blamed for the state I was in. I was beyond caring. I had just sat for two hours on my own poo—how much worse could it get?

When we got home, Anita told Mom. I had imagined the way it would play itself out. Mom would yell. I would go to the bathroom, dump my panties in the toilet, wipe my bum and then go to my room for a very long time.

Life can be surprising. She didn't yell. She just looked at me and didn't say a word. Then the kicker: she told Anita to take me to the bathroom and clean me up.

Mom probably wanted the nun to come and clean me up, but that wasn't going to happen. Mom knew even more than I did that there were some battles you just couldn't win. It didn't matter how many terrible things happened, you had to keep going. To stand up and ask, "What the hell have you done to my child?"—that would be a sign that all was not well; a crack would appear.

Our well-being depended on keeping up the pretense that there was order in all things, that God was good, that nuns and priests were good, and that they wanted only good for us. You couldn't shake too hard and have that whole facade come tumbling down. You might be calling into question what all the sacrifice and hard work were for. Next thing you know, we would stop going to church and confession. Mom and Dad would stop working at bingo. They would fire Dad from his job as janitor at the school, and then—well, you couldn't think about that. Mom knew all things were connected even if I just thought it was about shit.

~

Anita, Peter, Helena at their confirmation

What Have You Done for Me Lately?

While singing was rare at school, praying wasn't. We spent the largest part of each day praying. We prayed before school, before recess, after recess, before lunch, after lunch and before we went home. Those were just the everyday prayers. Sometimes when a fire truck went by we leapt to our feet and prayed for the poor souls whose house was burning. Those were my favourite. It was exciting to jump up and feel the blessed relief from sitting silently at a desk. "Hail Mary full of grace the Lord is with thee..." I shouted in grateful release.

Then there was Friday, when we could pray all morning, before confession and during mass. Church praying was easier because it was all in Latin and memorized and no one knew what we were saying. You just needed to chant along or just move your mouth and make noises. In those times there was only Latin, and no one cared that we had no idea what we were saying. The point of all this was not understanding but obedience. In fact, it was probably better that we didn't know we were planting the seeds of our own self-loathing.

I think we prayed mostly for forgiveness for being born evil and stained and horribly flawed. We begged for safety and succour. We begged not to go to the fiery pits of hell where our skin would be beaten from us and we would then face flaming torture. Forever. Alone. Forever.

Not seeing God, we were told, was going to be the really painful part of hell. This was the unbearable price for sin. We would never be in His divine presence. We would never feel the warm, fireplace glow of His love or be in the inner circle of those He really cared about. We would not be accepted and cherished like in that TV shows *Cheers*, "Where everybody knows your name."

I didn't buy it.

I already knew what it was like not being wanted, accepted or acknowledged. How bad could it be? I didn't really like Him anyway. He was bigger, stronger and meaner than anyone I knew. He was a bully. He was someone who could use His stunning power in any way He liked. He was a superhero gone wrong. Why would I want to spend forever, or even a day, with someone like that?

We didn't just pray for our own forgiveness. There were all those uninformed and uninitiated we included in our prayers, those who didn't have the great good luck to be born Catholic or to have chosen that divine path. We prayed, too, for the pagan babies all over the world. Those were the little babies who through no fault of their own had not received baptism before they died. I always pictured them just floating around, sad little smiles on their faces, waiting for us to send up enough prayers to redeem their unblessed souls. We prayed for the "fallen-away Catholics" who went to church only at Christmas and Easter and ate meat on Friday. We prayed for those who were living in sin. This included a list of bad things beyond measure. And of course we prayed for all those who had had, were currently having, were going to have or were even contemplating having unclean thoughts.

We prayed for those in Purgatory, that great waiting room in the sky where you were sent after you died if you still had some sin on your soul, like a port wine stain. Purgatory sins were really minor sins, like parking tickets. They were not as bad as the sins that got you a direct "Do-not-pass-Go" ticket to hell. Purgatory sins were sins you could have rid yourself of before you died if you had been thinking. But no, you had to die with them on your soul and now all of us here on Earth were saying prayers of penance for you. Slacker.

We should have saved a million souls. We should have paved our way to heaven with a guaranteed place of honour with all those hours of prayer. But we knew it wouldn't work, because we were so fundamentally flawed.

Still, there was always the faint hope held out to us in the form of confession. The trouble with confession was that at best it was a Band-Aid measure. It just didn't hold. Like making the bed or washing dishes or brushing your teeth, you had to keep doing it and doing it or you'd end up in the place you'd started with a heart blackened with sin.

Confession was not an optional item—"No, thank you, Sister. I think I'll give confession a miss today."

It is Friday morning. You go to confession. Even if you are six years old and can't even spell "confessional," you still must confess. Sure, you were baptized and got rid of that original sin, but that doesn't last forever. You slip back into evil behaviour. Even if you don't have a mortal sin to confess there are still the countless venial sins that need forgiveness. We were told the more frequently we received the sacrament the more able we would be to fight against our evil tendencies. We knew that those bad ways of being were just lurking around the corner like a sex offender about to flash us. Confession was supposed to make us more merciful, too. By recognizing our own wretchedness we could feel pity for other sinners fighting their own demons. It just scared the shit out of me.

I sat on those very hard, very smooth wooden benches and slid and slid on my navy-blue cotton panties with the elastic legs closer and closer toward that dark wooden box as big as two telephone booths. Frightening images of pain and suffering were everywhere. Way, way up Jesus hanging and bleeding on his cross. There was a gash in his side, a bleeding crown of thorns and huge nails in his feet and hands. The entire church should have been rated 14+.

Then it was my turn. Heart beating, mouth dry and barely able to swallow, I walked to the booth, stepped in, closed the door, sat down and pushed open the little screen.

"Bless me, Father, for I have sinned. It has been one week since my last confession...." There was a strong smell of old wood and beeswax candles and years of filtered incense, which should have been comforting and wasn't. I could see the shadowy silhouette of the priest and hear his breathing and sighing. I knew who it was—his name and what he looked like outside the box, with his black gown, white collar and tummy sticking out in front. I was fairly sure he knew who I was too, and that wasn't a good thing from my perspective. Of course he probably couldn't have cared less who I was—just one more little kid with one more string of silly sins—but I needed this to be over as quickly as possible before I bolted out of there.

If you were smart you prepared your sin list while you waited. Not too long a list, though. Just as three is the correct number in interior design, the optimum way to group candles and flowers, three is a good number of sins to recite. This number says, "I know I am a weak sinner, but I've got it under control."

You needed to be very careful with the types of sin you chose. You wanted the sins to seem real and not so trivial as to cause impatient sighs, and still not so horrible that the priest is left gasping and wondering how a child axe murderer got into his church, and would he get out of the confessional alive? Stealing cookies, swearing, using the Lord's name in vain, disobeying your parents—these were all good bets and would garner you a few Hail Marys, Our Fathers, a few decades of the rosary or, if the priest was in a bad mood, a few turns around the Stations of the Cross.

The Stations of the Cross sound ominous, and they were. In Latin they are aptly called *Via Dolorosa*, which means Way of Sorrows. In our church, there were fourteen three-dimensional sculptured tablets. These stations told a tale that got progressively more frightening the farther along you went. It began with Jesus being condemned to death and progressed to him carrying that great big cross, falling down many times, meeting his mother, the really gory nailing to the cross and, finally, his limp body taken down and laid in his mother's arms. You had to stand at each station and say a prayer and gaze up at the carnage. By the end you were exhausted from the scenes of brutality. This was the stuff of nightmares.

The whole confession experience was disturbing from start to finish. There is the terror of the confessional booth and then, because you are too little to have done anything of any consequence, you lie and end up feeling frightened at lying, to a priest, in God's house, while God was listening. I could practically hear the flames. The only blessing was that once the confession and its penance were over they were quickly forgotten—until next week.

For now, it was time to move on to mass and the real reason for confession: communion. Of all the sacraments, prayers, singing, kneeling, sitting, standing, reciting and general carrying on inside a Catholic church, the ritual of communion held the most cachet for kids. It was like a very formal buffet line-up without the salad bar. It was time-consuming and, most importantly, signalled that the end of mass was in sight.

It meant you could get up, shuffle sideways out of the pew and stand endlessly in line. You could watch as others knelt down with the underside of their shoes on display for you to note the wear, the holes and sometimes, if they were cheap shoes, the price written in red grease pen. Then it was your turn to kneel down, stick out your tongue, cross yourself, get up and, with your head piously lowered, walk back to your pew where you could now kneel down, put your head on your hands and, if you wanted to, doze off a little.

If you wanted to keep busy there was all the action around the wafer to attend to. It usually stuck to the roof of your mouth. You couldn't just jam your finger in there and pry it free. It was the transubstantiated body of Christ after all. Instead you had to worry away at it with your tongue without seeming to do that. Your mouth couldn't move and your cheeks couldn't bulge. You could stick your tongue to the roof of your mouth and melt it, or you could rub your tongue on it, gently, gently back and forth, until you worked it loose. By this time it should have melted to a soft, gooey pulp that was easy to swallow and, as far as being a food product, really worse than nothing. It reminded you how empty your stomach was from fasting; it was a long time since midnight. It was a brief reminder that waiting back at school was the piece of soggy toast and the boiled egg that you brought on Fridays to eat after mass. The truth was that I couldn't wait to eat it, even though the smell was disgusting and shameful and the other kids said, "Oh, who farted?"

Even though I had to sprinkle salt on it from a waxed-paper square, I still wanted it. It was my egg and my toast, and I was hungry.

Sometimes in the hiatus after receiving communion we watched the priest do his obsessive-compulsive display with the chalice, wiping it and wiping it and then folding the wiping cloth ever so carefully. Meanwhile I'd play a game with whoever was sitting next to me. I called it "Squeeze Hard."

In this game you took the other person's hand and squeezed it really hard. Then they slipped their hand out, leaving your hand in a claw-like pose. The next step involved stroking the bent hand. First you went over the fingers, then under the fingers, then back and forth along the wrist. I loved it. It created a sleepy, happy feeling. A few minutes of the rubbing and then the "frozen-handed" person carefully unfurled the now-very-stiff fingers. You did this slowly, one finger at a time to prolong the pleasure. You had to be careful, though; if you took too long the frozen effect wore off and all the squeezing and rubbing were for nothing. We always turned and looked at each other wide-eyed with surprise that it had happened again. When you're six years old, sitting on a hard bench for hours, bored beyond reason, this is your version of fun.

The weekly field trips to confess my sins were followed by the endless ritual of mass and made up a mosaic that was my school experience. Like a mosaic, up close it was just a lot of insignificant little pieces, but if you stood back you got the full, clear picture. It wasn't pretty.

In addition to masses, praying, singing and agony-filled confessions, there was also a buffet of feast days to fill our childhood time. I know that sometimes the Protestant kids who went to the public school down the block resented us and the fact that we had extra school days off. But they didn't have to get dressed up like folks from biblical times and carry life-sized statues around the block all the while praying and singing songs of praise.

At the time we were all thrilled with these events. We girls vied for the opportunity to wear the long, burgundy velvet dress with the matching velvet cape and cap. Against all odds my sister Anita was chosen for this privilege one year. She walked up so solemnly and placed her crown of flowers on the statue of the Blessed Virgin. "Oh Mary, we crown with roses today, Queen of the Angels, Queen of the May," we all sang happily.

Anita was beside herself with joy at this honour. Perhaps the memory of the floral coronation stands out for her because of its stark contrast to our usual mortifying lives at school. She suffered many small humiliations, unkind words from nuns, callous comments from Mom. These injuries and others, like water torture, wore away at her self-esteem but not her genuine nature. It seems the need to belong, to be accepted, to be deemed worthwhile cannot be extinguished no matter how terribly you are treated.

She does say she has a haunting suspicion she was chosen due to the pity vote. This was the year she lost her eye in an accident at home; a brother's curiosity and a BB gun pellet left under the ring on the stove had culminated in an explosion that pierced Anita's eye.

My mother used to recite that old rhyme, "Monday's child is fair of face, Tuesday's child is full of grace…" Well, Anita was Tuesday's child—sweet, kind, helpful and full of grace. The rhyme, however, neglects to say "unlucky." As though she were a magnet, bad things clung to her like many tiny, painful iron filings. Losing her eye was the zenith of her bad karma and its most dramatic.

I didn't know that the pellets inside a BB gun were made of copper. I didn't even know for sure what a BB pellet was. Peter did—he knew all about what fun they were and what they could do. The rest of us found out about copper when they tried to take the shattered pieces of one of those pellets from what was left of Anita's eye. The pellet had silently waited under the ring on the stove until Anita came up to add potatoes to the stew. There she stood, stirring and smiling and not knowing that just there was a piece of metal waiting to change her life. She was very surprised when it did explode and with the weird accuracy of a stealth bomber pierced her eye. She yelled and ran down the hall to look in the mirror that hung on the wall above the phone table. She took her hand off her eye and was shocked to see that her normal-sized pupil had become her whole eye.

We all knew we had to protect Peter, even though he had put that pellet there, along with lots of others, earlier, to see them explode. Most of them did, but not the one that was destined for Anita. So when I ran down the street to the store to get Mom and Dad I told them I didn't know what had happened to her. Anita offered a lie to explain why she was holding her hand over her eye, blood seeping through her fingers. "It was the potato peeler. It slipped while I was peeling the potatoes and it went into my eye."

My father swore; my mother grabbed Anita and looked closely at her and took her to the hospital. As bad as the pain in her eye was, Anita was more concerned with her gut. Her early and lifelong affair with stomach problems was already rearing its head. Nothing like losing your eye to cause the kind of stress that makes your stomach cramps go into overdrive. As Mom returned home, and Dad and Anita sat in that emergency room waiting to be seen, Anita was certainly aware of the smell of tension. Dad had already told her he had to get to bingo; he was in charge and needed to be there. Mom waited with the rest of us and was also thinking about bingo—some things are more important than others. There was going to be a party after bingo and they didn't want to miss that. At that point they had no idea what had really happened and that soon things would move out of the realm of impossible to possible.

A few days and several operations later, Mom and Dad came home without Anita. We stood and listened in a silent panic as Dad cried and told us the unbelievable. They couldn't save Anita's drowning eye. The metal shards were copper and couldn't be drawn out with a magnet. The eye was no longer an eye, just a mess of blood with all her beautiful hazel colour seeping into red. They were going to take out her ruined eye and leave a dark, wet hole where it used to be. She would "lose" her eye.

Who loses an eye? You lose shoes and socks, not eyes. In a world where your sister could misplace her eye, the incredibly rare and frightening sight of Dad crying was just as it should be. It signalled that something was definitely very wrong. The world had tilted.

Other things happened that day. Peter was punished, probably hit with Dad's thick, brown belt. Today he would have received counselling for the trauma he must have experienced when he realized the unbelievable result of just being a stupid kid.

After they took her eye away and replaced it with nothing, Anita spent a few days in hospital recovering from something she would never recover from. Peter went to visit her. Anita was twelve and Peter was fifteen. He had brought a plastic play gun with him.

"Go ahead, shoot me," he said to her. "It actually doesn't work, but maybe you can just point it at me and pull the trigger and maybe you would feel like you shot me."

Anita told him for the first time of many times, "It's okay; it was an accident." He never believed her.

When she came home from the hospital we still shared the same bedroom and bunk beds. Now she was on the bottom; in case she rolled over in the night she wouldn't have as far to fall. She wore a black eye patch, which partially obscured the bruising that is caused when you take out an eye. I asked her if it hurt but I didn't really want to know. The whole thing was disgusting and scary and reminded me that terrible things can happen to anyone for no reason. I was just glad it wasn't me. I still am.

Mom, who was always afraid that if you gave even a little sympathy the receiver would keep on demanding more, said, "Don't think you're going to get special treatment just because you lost an eye." Dad said nothing.

Anita didn't get a new eye right away. She wore the black eye patch to cover up the curved white, plastic disk used as a shape-holder in her useless eye socket. Then began the long, ongoing process of finding just the right false eye.

The eye guy had a big chest that opened up like a fishing tackle box. There were rows and rows of prosthetics, lined up in black velvet drawers, shaded from deepest darkest black to the palest of pale blue eyes. They stared up at us, lifeless bits of plastic waiting to be animated.

In the beginning the eye never fit right. Her eyelid sagged, and her eye socket oozed its sad tears of loss. Unseen walls and doors left cuts and bumps. A strategically placed whack caused her eye to pop out and roll like a crazy marble across the floor.

It popped out once when we were in high school. We were at a public school, our first foray into the world of non-Catholics. I was in Grade 9 and Anita in Grade 10. She loved public school. She was popular. She had friends, and boys wanted to walk her home. I hated it, and her for being so happy.

In the high school washroom together one day, Anita ducked into the stall to give her socket a rest. It always hurt and tiny specks of dirt caused it to sting and burn. She took out her eye and it slipped from her hand and rolled under the stall door. Like a penny it rolled and rolled and finally came to rest in the middle of the washroom floor. No one noticed it at first. Then, one of the girls saw it and said, "Oh, my God, look at that—is that an eye?"

The mature and kind thing to do would have been to go over and pick it up and pass it under to Anita, to make a connection with her to let her know she wasn't alone. I wanted to just slip out and pretend I had nothing to do with the glass eye staring up at us. Without looking at anyone I walked over to it, nudged it sideways with my foot and sent it skittering under the washroom stall. Anita didn't make a sound. And then I walked out.

If she was sad or angry or frustrated we didn't know. Today she would be labelled disabled and given a special teacher, a modified curriculum, preferential seating in a classroom and an Individual Education Plan. Instead she went to Our Lady of Sorrows and offered her pain and shock, her embarrassment and sadness up to the Virgin Mary.

Around the same time as Anita's lost eye we became the beneficiaries of someone's generosity and were sent off to the Catholic summer camp as charity cases. You read a lot about children's sad adventures at camp—how they miss home, the food is so awful and they miss their own bed. We had those same feelings wrapped up in daily reminders that we wouldn't be there if it weren't for the largesse of others.

We didn't want to be at Star of the Sea. We would like to have stayed at home and hung out together, getting up to absolutely nothing. Instead we yet again had to go to church, except now we had to walk miles to get there, and there were even more rules here than at school. There were rigid times to go to bed and get up. The lights went out whether you were afraid of the dark or not, and you had chores to do—just like at home, only there were more of them. And of course we ate unspeakable food in which Jell-O figured largely. We ate all our meals in a huge hall with people we didn't know. The tables were covered with oilcloth, which was always slightly sticky and smelled like a dirty dishrag.

As usual I was always in trouble. Even a marshmallow roast, which should have been a bright spark in the week, turned into a disaster. Some kid, obviously a "paying guest," stuck a flaming marshmallow onto my arm. It was so hot it took away a piece of my skin. I saw the damage, which naturally made me scream long and loud. The nun yelled at me for being a baby.

"You should watch where you fling your arms. Can't you see there are hot marshmallows being roasted?"

Well, yes, actually; I did see them. I just wasn't expecting one to land up on my arm. Anita stepped in to defend me because that is just what she did, and she was punished for her trouble. All in all it was the camp from hell, and both of us couldn't wait to get home.

When it was suggested the following summer that we might like to go to camp again, we very politely said, "No, thanks, Mom. We would rather stay home with you and help around the house."

We were desperate. Mom seemed just a bit doubtful, but hey—she wasn't going to turn down offers of household help. And believe me, she held us to it.

Anita says that being chosen to sing "You Are My Sunshine" for the archbishop when he visited the camp one day and wearing that velvet gown while crowning the statue of the Virgin Mary are her best early-childhood memories.

For me, childhood memories are more about an absence of things. A good day for me was no nun yelling, shouting or berating me to do or not do something. No ratty little kid at school calling me names like "Garbage Can," which doesn't exactly rhyme with Gojević but did make a none-too-subtle reference to Dad's janitor job.

Objects in Mirror Are Closer than They Appear

The best part of my birthdays was the fact that on that one day a year I didn't have to do anything. No chores, no dishes, no potatoes, no minding babies—just a blissful nothing. Yes, there was cake and ice cream and everyone sang the birthday song to you, but it was that vast expanse of a day spreading ahead with no tasks that was a kind of paradise. If you had asked Mom to describe us, she would have reported in her shorthand way that "Pauline is the laziest of the lot; she's always hiding somewhere trying to avoid work." She was right. I just wanted to be left alone. But there was no being left alone anywhere.

Anita and I do share one deliriously joyous memory. It came just as we were leaving our childhood behind. It was a Christmas season that began, like many others, with Dad's almost manic decorating. He had a penchant for sparkly, glittery, multicoloured garlands, which he looped everywhere. You had to look carefully to ensure you didn't walk into one and get strangled. He was also a very big fan of Snow In a Can. He divided the sides of the large front window into panes using black electrical tape, artfully drew snow in every square and then wrote "Merry Christmas" in large snow letters in the middle of the window. He did it backwards so it read correctly from the outside. I always thought that trick was a bit silly since we were inside reading it, but I certainly wasn't going to share my observation with Dad.

When it came to Christmas decorations he was the king. Besides, it was rare to see him so happy and having fun; when he was happy we were happy. He also liked to swoop some Asian-influenced shiny, metallic accordion streamers from which he would suspend all the Christmas cards. The house was awash in decorations as if a crazed elf with no style had been chosen as our personal Christmas designer.

Dad went on to make a big cedar bough for the front door tied with a huge red ribbon. He called them cedar "buffs," and for many years I thought that's what they were. I probably just thought the word inside my head, but one day I must have used it quite naturally in conversation, as in, "When I have my own apartment I am definitely going to put a cedar buff on my door." You never forget how to pronounce a word you learn through embarrassment.

In many Christmas magazines today you read about families going out to choose just the perfect tree, chopping it down and stopping for a steaming mug of hot chocolate before gleefully carrying the tree home to decorate in a frenzy of family fun. In our case Dad brought home a tree as close to Christmas as he could possibly get. We always said, "Dad, this is the best tree we've ever had," even if we did have to cut branches off the top to get it in the living room and then tie those branches to the bare spots. Sometimes the trunks of a tree would be so badly twisted that no amount of swearing, tilting or tipping would make it stand up. Those years Dad would put a hook in the wall and we'd tie the tree to it. It worked.

As kids we just wanted to throw big clumps of tinsel on the tree. Fortunately for us, neither Mom nor Dad was all that committed to an artfully decorated tree and just let us have our way. We always kept our tree up until January 6, the Epiphany, when the wise men were supposed to have finally arrived, better late than never, at the manger. By then the tree would be a tinder-dry fire hazard and most of the needles would have fallen off and be lying around the base of the tree's white cloth of snow. We were always glad to see it go, like an out-of-town guest who had stayed just a few days too long. And the presents were gone, so, really, what was the point?

When I think about Christmas and presents and Mom and Dad, I try to imagine to what lengths they must have gone so they could put anything under the tree. One way they managed was by adhering to rules about the Christmas presents. They were explained to us like this: "Each of you will get one slightly larger present and then a few small ones, depending on how things go, and of course your stocking." Some Christmases you would have been hard pressed to call any of our presents "larger," but there was always something, and no matter how deep your disappointment it was considered very bad form to say anything but "Thank you."

One Christmas I stepped outside the bounds of good behaviour and sulked about my present. Or maybe I was upset because in my opinion I didn't get enough. I didn't say anything, but my face might have shown the true depth of my feelings. My father was not amused, and yelled what he often said at Christmas time when he was angry: "Don't make me hit you on your Christmas day!" I was sent to my room.

Helena as usual tried to smooth it all over and acted as a go-between. She asked me what was wrong and then she would tell Dad a more palatable version of what I had said. I must have been angry but feeling like a jerk, too, because I knew how unreasonable I was being. In the darkening light of a late Christmas afternoon I sat on my bunk bed and held the doll I had received but didn't want and mumbled how unfair everything was, how mean my parents were, how I wasn't ever coming out of my room. It wasn't the first time in my life I behaved badly, or the last, but it sticks with me as a particularly unflattering event even though I was just a kid.

Perhaps it is still vivid because it was so very much out of the realm of behaviour we were all so good at maintaining. Strict adherence to "the code of compliance" is what kept the machinery of the family if not humming along then at least running. I wish that memory wasn't lodged so deeply; I would love to get rid of it. But bad memories are the real stickers. They are the ones you can conjure up with great detail, including the smells in the room and what you were wearing. No doubt if I succumb to some kind of dementia, that will be the damn memory that will remain. It has, as they say, legs.

I think the really sad thing about getting older—besides wrinkles, sagging breasts, batwing arms and hot flashes—is that it gets harder to be truly surprised by anything. Being surprised is just one of the joys of youth. And so it was that one amazing Christmas morning Anita and I were both splendidly, unexpectedly surprised. For two young teenagers, receiving fashionable clothes that fit for Christmas was a miracle like the loaves and fishes. But there they were: Anita's blue and my red glorious, corduroy bell-bottom pants. We screamed, we shrieked, we ran around in circles. Most of our clothes were one or two years behind the current fashion, so to receive clothes that were of the moment was more than surprising—it was fabulous.

But wait, there's more. We were also given matching stripped turtleneck tops to go with those amazing pants and, most wonderful of all, white go-go boots. There have been very few times in our lives when we were so happy. Here we were at last, in style. We put on all our finery and marched right down to the busiest street near our house and walked up and down, our little chests stuck out, our wide bell-bottom pants flapping, smiling to each other and to every car that passed by, thinking, *"Yes, this is it—we've made it."* There aren't any pictures of us in those outfits. It doesn't matter. In fact, it might be better that way.

∼

B. Pauline, Helena, Mom (with John) Peter, Anita
F. Tony, Eileen – 1957

But Can You Clean?

At three o'clock we lined up in our classrooms to go home for the day. Dad waited on the other side of the door in his army-green trousers and matching shirt. He would just look at one of my brothers or sisters or me and cock his head with a silent "Come here." You'd leave the line and stand beside him, staring down, rigidly still, while the others filed out.

He had his tools all ready. There was the large garbage can, a big dust mop and a kid-sized, brown-handled brush lined up waiting. We knew what to do.

Most often you cleaned your own classroom first while it was still warm from all the other kids and the nun was still in there. Dad's big mop wouldn't fit under the rows of desks, which were nailed to runners, so we went to the front of the row where we crouched down and did a little slide-hop dance, inching along like strong little chimps. Our crummy Catholic uniforms dragged in the dust and our droopy socks, held up with elastic bands, dug into our calves while we swept the dust from under the desks to a small pile at the ends. Dad would come with his mop and sweep all the small piles into one big pile. This large pile was picked up with a big, black, metal dustpan and dumped into the garbage can. We did this in all the classrooms. The nuns in each of the rooms pretended we weren't there, even when we went under their desks to clean.

Sometimes one of us would go downstairs and use the big mop and sweep the large, open, cement-floored area used for indoor play. This was fun because you could stand up and run with the mop as you went back and forth.

Not everyone had to stay every day. If there was a schedule I don't remember it, but I do know that sometimes you could plead your case before school and then Dad would say, "Okay, then tell Eileen she has to stay." Switching didn't make you popular and was seen by most of us as cheating.

Psychologists will talk about the damage that humiliating a child can have on their future development. For true psychic damage you need to combine shame with guilt and embarrassment; they are the true trifecta of emotional scarring. I wondered what it would be like to just go home after school like other kids. I knew there were children who lived lives like that. They didn't have to clean up other peoples' dirt. There were kids who didn't have to pretend not to be ashamed of their father, who was so desperate he needed his children to help him do his work.

The nuns liked having the Gojević family around. It gave them opportunities to practise public forbearance. But privately they loved being able, with every sideways glance, with every punishment, with every remark, to let us know we just weren't good enough. There were too many of us. We were noisy and messy with uniforms that didn't quite fit and had mismatched socks. We reminded them of the world and all its complications, its confusion and choices and its furious goings on. Somewhere men and women were fornicating and creating children. They wanted their blessed peace and quiet in their dark house next to the school.

It was inevitable that their world and ours would collide, although their campaign of meanness and disrespect toward us was subtle. They practised subterfuge and cunning and they hurt us in many small, almost unseen ways, like a hundred paper cuts that barely bleed but cause intense, throat-catching pain.

Maybe it was the labour of getting dressed each day that contributed to their sour mood. They were covered with white coifs that hid their hair, and then there were the headbands and wimples and veils and tunics and heavy, highly detailed crucifixes that hung around their necks. If you were being disciplined, these could be a focus of attention. We used to challenge each other to try to touch the very tip of their veil as they swept by, storming and swanning around the room.

The nuns seemed to come in two shapes: thin and fat. The thin ones had bony hands and sunken cheeks and deep, deep wrinkles. The fat ones looked like they should have been jolly. One of them was so fat she couldn't go down the aisle straight. She had to shuffle down sideways puffing, red-faced and angry as she called out the spelling list. She liked to use the list as an opportunity to teach lessons on social structure and the class system.

"Tissue." (She pronounced it "tiss-you.") Then she used it in a sentence.

"The student used a tiss-you when blowing her nose and didn't wipe it on her arm."

Or "Paper"—"The mother sent a note to school written on good-quality writing paper." This, directed at me since she had told me that morning how disappointed she was with the note, written on a piece of scrap paper, I had brought from my mother.

When she came down the aisle she was so close we were presented with a perfect opportunity to touch her veil. There was some fear that in touching it you might feel a sudden sharp shock or—more horrible—you would get caught touching that most sacred garment. We tried to do it anyway. We were brave and filled with excitement at the thrill of the hunt. I actually did it once and was disappointed at the lack of any sudden zing of electricity and the sheer boring nothingness of it.

Sometimes the nuns would lean against the blackboard and come away with whatever spelling list or math problems there had been now appearing in reverse on their black habits. An alternate universe was written there large and clear. There was something intensely satisfying about those smudges, especially as the nuns walked around not knowing how very human they appeared even for a brief period of time.

For the most part we just took what was handed out because we knew there was really no alternative. They were the "servants of God." There was no use in complaining about unfairness or plain mean-spirited behaviour.

It needs to be said that under pressure lots of things can happen. Bottles explode, mountains erupt and continents are formed. Small children are a bit like nature under pressure. It seems you can push and shove them a lot but then they, too, react. A nun telling me I couldn't leave the room to sing in the choir created just such an occasion for me. I threw a blackboard brush and it grazed her habit. It didn't happen in slow motion. In fact it was a swift-moving arc, too quick to really appreciate. It would have been great to see the instant slo-mo replay as the brush moved through the air and hit her habit, causing her to wince slightly as the chalk billowed around and fell in a dusty cloud to the ground.

She saw my upraised arm and my overhand girl pitch. It was just one of the times in my life when I wished I were more athletic. I wanted to hit her in the face with the brush and cause blood to stream down. I wanted her to yelp in pain and surprise. I wanted to see her look of shock and disbelief. I had to settle for the general in-drawn breath in the classroom.

Before a judge I would have pleaded "crime of passion." That would have been a lie, because those kinds of crimes are not supposed to be premeditated. They happen in the excitement of the moment, whereas I had dreamed about inflicting pain on any one of those nuns for a long, long time. However, in my dreams I never got beyond the pain I caused to what would happen to me next.

She stopped, looked at me, paused for just a millisecond and said, "Go get your father."

This wasn't the first time that punishment began by getting Dad. As our school custodian he was always somewhere near by. I spent the time it took trying to find him thinking of ways to casually say, "I hit the nun with a blackboard brush and she'd like to talk to you."

There was no way to say that and make it sound normal. I found him mopping a floor, and when I said the nun wanted to see him he threw the mop handle down hard. It wasn't necessary to tell him why he needed to come. It didn't really matter what I'd done. I was wrong and I would pay. He swore in Croatian about women's body parts. I didn't know he was talking about women's body parts at the time. That information came later when my brothers, who were interested in all things sexy, found out what Dad was saying every time he swore.

When we got back to the classroom we both had to go up to the front of the room.

"Mr. Go-jev-ik, Pauline has once again been rude, but this time she has gone beyond the beyond. Tell your father and the whole class what you have done!"

"I threw the blackboard brush," I whispered.

"Speak louder, you terrible girl, and tell your father everything," she shrieked.

"I threw the black board brush... hard." I shouted, "But she wouldn't let me go to choir"—I continued building up an indignant steam—"and I love to go to choir and Mom said I could go to choir and she"—I indicated the nun with a wave of my shaking hand—"said I had to stay here and do math and I told her...." I ran out of steam and courage.

"Mr. Go-je-vik," she repeated very slowly through clenched teeth, "she hit me with the brush. She insulted me and the body of Christ, of which we are all a part." She finally stopped. She had said all this very quietly while standing very rigidly, arms by her sides, staring straight ahead. It struck me as amazing that she could be so still and yet have so much power and venom in her voice.

Looking back I wish I had been sitting in the class watching this whole scene transpire. Everything you needed for good drama was there: fury, passion, fear and someone else in a horrible position. No one in that room would ever have to go get their father in the middle of the day, bring them back to their classroom and admit the stupid thing they had done. And it wasn't enough that I was mortified. I had to be the source of my father's humiliation too. My father's response was brief and to the point.

"I apologize for her, Sister. I will punish her when we get home."

He would punish me—not talk to me, not deal with me, not give me a consequence. No, he would punish me, which was of course exactly what she wanted.

To me he said, "Is this the way your mother and I have brought you up? Apologize."

He spoke in a normal tone of voice. It was that voice that really scared me. Like millions of kids before me I said I was sorry and wasn't. Then my father left the room and I returned to my seat to spend the rest of the afternoon thinking about what was going to happen when I got home.

I hadn't been hit with the strap that many times. My brother Peter was definitely the reigning champ in that area. But you don't easily forget a thick brown belt and what it can do to the back of your legs and bum. That strap left big, red welts that took some time to calm down and sometimes left bruises. Those bruises could be tricky to explain. It's not good to be hit by your father, but it also is not good for others to know about it. I was frightened at the pain I knew was coming, but being pissed at that nun distracted me.

He did hit me, but rather half-heartedly. I think he would rather have hit that nun. While he was hitting me he said, "Why did you make me do this?"

I don't think he meant, "Why did you make me hit you?" I think he meant, "Why did you make me have to come to that room and stand in front of that class and have that bitch berate us both? Why did you have to remind me I am just a janitor and I have to take shit from some frustrated, angry, evil woman?" I forgave my father for hitting me. There are some things worse than the belt.

∼

Pero Anton Gojević

Jack-of-All-Trades....

Before my father met my mother in England, married her, had five children, came to Canada and had seven more, he was a university-educated ship's captain. He spoke several languages and knew about places like Rio de Janeiro and South Africa. He was trim and fit with huge forearms like Popeye's, short legs for a relatively tall man and thick, dark, wavy hair that he brushed back from a broad, washboard forehead. He had smooth olive skin, a chin as square as Superman's, and dark, dark, deep-set eyes. In old black-and-white photographs of him leaning up against a ladder with his hands in his loose-fitting European-cut pants he looked like a movie star. He was born in Croatia, which was so far away to us that it existed like heaven: only in the imagination. You just had to take it on faith that it was there. He spoke of that far-off magical place longingly but not often.

Dad was never warm in Canada. Even in the height of summer when everyone one else complained and said the heat was unbearable and what they wouldn't do for rain, he would sigh, "This is a bit better." He spoke about swimming in the warm, blood-heated water from the village abattoir as it rushed down to the Adriatic Sea and how happy he was swimming in its pinky foam.

His name was Pero; Peter in English. Of course he didn't change his name to Peter. He wouldn't change the strange spelling of our last name so it could be pronounced or spelled either. While all around him immigrants were changing their names, he refused. He even kept the accent over the "c," which indicated the pronunciation "ich."

"What's so hard they can't learn "c" with an accent means ich?" He spoke English well if your definition was using correct syntax and having a rich if not-always-appropriate vocabulary, but not if it needed to be accent-free. My friends all said, "How do you understand him? I can't make out a word he says."

I heard an accent, I guess, but it was as much a part of him as the constant sweaty man smell he always had about him. He thought that showering more than once a week was somehow unhealthy. "All that washing, you send your body oils down the drain. A wicked waste," he said.

He shouted and swore a lot in Croatian. He didn't seem to need sleep. He worked day and night doing jobs he was overqualified for and for which he was poorly paid, among them painting bridges, even though he hated heights. He wanted to be independent in his new country but never really was. And he had a frightening but not unpredictable temper because he lived in a constant state of exhaustion, nerves raw and exposed.

The worst time to make him angry was at the dinner table. There were so many things to throw. Here is an image of a large roast he picked up and threw at a wall, the force so great it sticks there and hangs for a microsecond and then in slow motion slides down the wall, leaving behind a slightly bloody trail. All of us are watching its journey very quietly. He seemed to feel better after that. The roast was brought back, he sliced it and we ate it. It was like that—quick bursts of fireworks and then everything carried on as if nothing had happened.

Eggs were a common morning-time projectile. These were raw eggs for the most part, thrown just as breakfast was starting. Dad was often cranky and volatile in the morning, and these eggs were close at hand. An impressive variation was the throwing of fried eggs. They didn't make quite the same satisfying "thunk" on the wall, but they made a good, solid splat and left an unholy mess, which the person who had caused the anger in the first place had to clean up.

He wasn't an easy man, or a calm man or even, I suspect, a happy man, but he was so easy to love. We all knew that in spite of all his fearsome failings he was a lover. He was exuberant with his affection. He was as generous with his hugs and kisses as he was with his spectacular displays of temper. He had vast reserves of energy, passion and, although he wasn't often allowed to display it, wisdom.

Here was a man who defined multitasking before that word became popular. When he wasn't sweeping floors and scrubbing out toilets at our school or running the bingo he was also our gym teacher. I have no idea what possible qualifications he could have had for this job. It's true he did seem strong and healthy. Perhaps it was a nod to his education, although how being trained to be a ship's captain prepares you to work in physical education was not clear. There probably just wasn't anyone else who would do it for free. The nuns certainly weren't going to do it. Their only physical exercise seemed to be giving the strappings once weekly. That might build up their biceps, but you would worry about their cardiovascular capabilities.

He liked teaching those PE classes. It appealed to his sense of order. We would all line up and march over to the church hall, next to the school, which doubled as our gym. Most of our classes consisted of rope climbing, jumping jacks and running around the hall. I was always a little surprised that the kids in my class and the other classes did what he told them to do. It just shows how very compliant we all were. I remember a brief sensation of pride that it was my Dad teaching phys ed. I doubt he felt any pride about me. My physical prowess extended to three very-red-faced jumping jacks and hanging onto the knot at the end of the climbing rope, my arms extended upwards as far as they would go in an attempt to give the appearance of someone going up a rope.

Fortunately for Dad, other members of the family were a lot more physically adept than I. Anita could run like there was no tomorrow, and all the others gave doing as he asked a very good shot. I wanted to, but somehow I lacked not only the physical prowess but the mental agility too. I never have been able to push myself to do things that ultimately were not satisfying in the vague hope that somehow, if I just pushed myself harder, I too some day would be a star of something. You could call that a character flaw. I prefer to think of it as being smart enough to know when to say "Uncle."

Given enough training, time and, importantly, money, Anita might have gone on to do great things athletically. That wasn't the way our lives worked. Our single biggest tie was to our home. It formed the apex of the triangle that included school and church. That was it. That was our world. No traipsing off to after-school running practice, no ice-skating lessons or ballet or gymnastics or any of the thousand and one things kids got up to. Not for us; no, we went straight home to do any one of a million things Mom dreamed up for us to do, or we stayed at school as part of the cleaning brigade.

In essence it meant we spent most of our childhood lives within the walls of our home or our backyard doing our parents' bidding. Can you call us dutiful when that is all we knew? It didn't occur to us that we could rebel, say "No," be disrespectful or try to forge a new path. Mom and Dad held total and complete control. Looking back, I see the dearth of opportunities and experiences that lifestyle created. But then, that was just the way it was. It was pointless and ultimately futile to talk about what some other kid's family did and why couldn't we.

Within the confines of our house we had our own little universe that ran by its own rules. To the disciplinary mix Mom brought consistency and Dad brought power and fear. We knew we would *always* get into trouble for arguing with each other. There would never be a time when Mom and Dad would look at each other and with a chuckle say, "Aren't they cute," and then go on to say, "Come on, now, children; behave yourselves." They never missed an opportunity to show us just how sincere they were about our behaviour. Punishment was swift and often painful. Dad was usually the enforcer. He could whip his thick, brown belt off his pants with lightning speed and use it to great effect.

There was, however, one epic battle between Mom and I. I seem to remember it involving me throwing a large silver platter at Peter, causing major damage to the platter and not Peter. Probably if it had connected and beaned him instead of knocking a little silver stub off the platter it all wouldn't have escalated to quite the extent it did. Mom was furious at me and came at me with the wooden spoon. From unknown sources came a burst of energy and I took off. This notion of escaping was a completely foreign one for all us. Running away from punishment was unheard of. You stood there. You took it. Not this time, though. I wasn't really surprised when Mom followed, yelling about what would happen when she got me. I was deaf to her threats. I raced into the dining room, Mom hot on my heels. Like cartoon characters we ran around that table; you could almost hear the crazy soundtrack playing.

I stopped on one side and glared at her; she yelled and tried to reach over to me but the gap was too wide. I knew this was going to end badly for me and that I had made an error in bolting. Usually the best thing is to just stand still, take it, get it over with and go off and sulk. But having taken this foolish route I was forced to continue.

She yelled, I yelled back. She threw the wooden spoon at me. I ducked. I eventually made a dash for the door and ran upstairs to the bedroom. I had tired her out but I knew what was coming—the words every kid fears, especially us: "You wait until your father comes home." This was in fact not a threat but a promise.

If Dad did punish me when he came home (and I am fairly certain that he must have) I don't remember. What is still so clear in my mind was that one time I stood up to Mom. It felt good, but obviously not good enough, because in all the time I was a child that was my single attempt at rebellion.

In my case the hitting stopped when I was twelve. Who knows what I had done that time but it resulted in Dad slapping me hard across the face. There was nothing unusual there. The strange thing is what happened next. Mom came in and saw a complete imprint of Dad's hand: bright red, swollen and hinting at the bruising that was to come.

"Pero," she shouted, "now she will have to stay home. We can't send her to school like that." Just like Vegas, what happened at home stayed at home.

That was the last time Dad hit me. I believe he really did feel badly about what he had done. Of course he never said so and I never expected him to. It was enough for me that it didn't happen again.

Popular psychology states that we tend to raise our children the way we were raised. In Mom and Dad's case I am sure that was true. Dad told us an apocalyptic story about his mother. He was a very young boy, three or four. During the day he had done something wrong. He didn't remember what he had done—most children don't; they just remember the outcome. This particular time he thought his punishment was being sent to bed. But no, there was more to come. There is that little boy fast asleep. His mother wakes him up and gives him several good slaps.

"You will remember not to do .... ever again," his mother screamed at him in a rage. "Now go back to bed."

She told him the next day that she wanted to impress upon him the evil of his ways and that if she had just hit him when he'd done the deed he wouldn't have remembered and taken it to heart. Waking him up hours later was meant to sear the memory permanently and so ensure he would never do it again, whatever "it" was. What he could always recall, all those years later, was the fear and absolute horror at being woken from a sound sleep to feel her hands slapping him over and over.

And yet when he shared this object lesson with us he never berated his mother. In fact, he usually told this story with just a hint of pride in his voice.

"Now there was a woman with pride. She was willing to do the hard thing."

I think we were meant to infer that he, too, was doing the hard thing, the thing he would rather not do. It is true that after whatever punishment he had meted out he didn't linger in that anger. You did your bad thing. He did his bad thing. Life went on.

Not so with Mom, who could and did hold grudges for a lifetime. Every bad thing you ever did was stored away in her grudge bank, gaining interest just in case you ever got it in your head to do something like that again. She would bring up the last time you did that terrible thing with remarkable accuracy: dates, times—it was all there. From this litany of mistakes she built up a picture of who you were, and she never let it go.

"You always lie," she would say to one. "You always cheat," she'd say to another. "I can never trust you," was hurled at someone else. "You are so lazy; you never do your fair share."

On and on she would go. In her opinion we all had our particular fatal flaws. Years later as adults she would still recount these tales of weakness and wrongdoing. She took our childish behaviour as a personal affront to her dignity. Here she was trying to create order out of chaos and all we did was thwart her at every turn. Shameful. Like signs in a big-box store, those mini-characterizations she created acted as guideposts for her dealings with us. Unlike Dad, who really believed that the fairest approach was to treat us all the same, Mom did know us, in her way, as individuals. Unfortunately for us she clung to her one-dimensional creations, never allowing for the fact that we were growing, changing and becoming much more than her one-line description. In the face of that diversity she decided to reduce us to manageable terms. It must have been hard to love all those labels.

∼

B. Tony, Pauline, Anita, Peter, Helena, Eileen
F: Kathleen, Mum (with Mary Anne) Dad (with Brendan), Mike and John

Once Upon A Time

There's a crisp black-and-white photo of us together taken in the early '60s. The first thing that strikes you about that picture is all the big eyes staring out; some to the left, some to the right, everybody looking for their own anchor. Then you might notice that there are eleven children in that picture along with Mom and Dad: Helena, Peter, Anita, Pauline, Eileen, Tony, John, Kathleen, Michael, Mary Anne and Brendan. The smallest are sitting on Mom and Dad's knees and the rest of us are arranged like Maruschka dolls, standing nice and straight just like we were told. There were a hell of a lot of us, and there was the picture to prove it.

We all look so clean and polished, boys in shirts and ties, girls in dresses. Seconds before that shot was taken Dad was shouting at someone about something. That explains the broad range of expressions from smiling to truly sad. This was a studio picture taken by a real photographer, so he probably managed to lighten the whole thing up and get at least some of us to say "Cheese." The young ones come across as cute, with girls in their little dresses and boys with a collection of vests, bow ties and shorts. The older ones looked resigned.

I have a hairdo I am sure I created myself. I don't know what look I was trying to achieve. My hair was short at this point and my bangs are three inches above my eyebrows. I had backcombed the top of my hair to give it height. It looks like I have stuck a toupee on top of my head, because underneath this fashionable nest my hair is shorter than my brothers'. I'm wearing a dress appropriate for a thirty-year-old, with three big buttons down the front and a belt that is right under my armpits. I am eleven years old.

There aren't a lot of pictures of any of us at that time. Probably just as well or there would be many more pictures of shameful hairdos and outfits. Cameras and film were a luxury and, anyway, we didn't know it was important to capture that swift-moving time; it seemed to be moving so sluggishly.

If anyone had looked at that picture they might have seen eleven hopeful children with just as much chance for happiness and good health and success as the kids down the street. Just goes to show, doesn't it?

Peter, for example, the second-born child, is wearing a snappy sport jacket, white shirt and fashionably narrow tie. He is smiling a closed-mouth, tilted smile. He was probably planning his next heist. He was around sixteen years old and just beginning his long, rather unsuccessful career as a criminal. He began very young and got more desperate as he got older. The signs were all there, but who could believe that living among us like a shadow, like an alien from Mars, was a thief and liar. He didn't discriminate in any way. He stole from anyone, amounts small and large. He got into kinds of things none of us knew anything about. I didn't really want to get too close to him in case I ended up like him. And I had my own problems trying to navigate the strange world we lived in.

Peter was named after Dad. He was strong and healthy, smart and handsome. But if you asked Mom she would tell you, "He looked like a skinned rabbit when they brought him to me in the hospital after he was born. He was so long, and slimy and red-looking. Not a beautiful, chubby baby like Helena." And that was that. I guess she didn't like rabbits and it is hard to bond with a long, red, slimy thing.

He may have had Dad on his side in the beginning. Dad had wanted a boy, after all, and here was a miniature version of him. Peter didn't cry a lot as a baby—if he did, Mom would definitely have told everyone—so it couldn't have been colic that turned her off. She told them about his other transgressions though. He didn't listen to her and come when he was called, he made a mess, and he got dirty all the time after she had just dressed him up in a cute little sailor suit.

Mom and Dad were still in England, and Dad wasn't home very much during the first year of Peter's life, so his main definer was Mom. She didn't paint glowing pictures of him to Dad when he returned from sea. Instead, she recounted a long list of why he was not the boy of her dreams. Peter never told me this or any of the other sad things that happened to him as a child. That has always been Helena's job. She has always explained him to us and to some extent to himself.

So he had a mom who wasn't thrilled with him and a dad who didn't know him. Like a textbook case of wish fulfillment, he turned out to be the kind of boy Mom said he was: a difficult, naughty little troublemaker.

Things didn't improve as he got older. He learned early how to steal but never figured out how not to get caught. He stole from Mom's purse and she caught him. He stole from stores and they caught him. But even more than stealing he liked to burn things. He was, in the beginning, at least, a better arsonist than he was a thief.

One very cold morning at eight years of age, he decided that setting a fire in a house we were renting in Maillardville would warm things up. It was certainly a worrisome precursor of fiery things to come. This particular fire started out small enough. It was a little nothing, really, in a broom closet. In fact, it was so small Mom thought she could play fire fighter and put it out. Of course she didn't count on the incendiary effect of shoe polish and rags, and before she knew it the thing was out of hand.

This small French enclave just outside of Vancouver had only a volunteer fire department. After what was forever they arrived to find that the water in the pipes was frozen. The heat was amazing as we stood and watched the house burn to the ground and the windows explode. Rings, pictures, papers, silver, clothes—all gone. Everything, which wasn't much really, that we had brought with us from England—gone.

Mom may have felt this loss most keenly. Not only had she left her family in England—a family she would not return to for twenty years—but now all her tangible English memories were gone too. Dad, who had left his Croatian homeland years before, had learned what it felt like to travel light. For him, the loss of the house was much more about shelter for his family, even if there were only six children to worry about at this time.

There was a picture in the local paper of all of us lined up wearing borrowed clothes, since we had escaped in our pyjamas. I am smiling, which seems strange to me—force of habit, I guess. I am wearing a boy's t-shirt and pants with the fly down. The story the paper ran said the fire was a result of "spontaneous combustion." Just like those saints who burst into flames out of love for God. And that was the story Mom and Dad went with.

The word got out to the Croatian community that we were homeless, and we were housed in the basement of a family that knew Dad. It was a bit crowded, and even at four years old I felt that odd sensation you get when you know you are a charity case. You have to speak very quietly, no loud noises allowed, and say "Thank you" with every second breath.

Then a miracle happened. An old lady died, leaving her unmarried daughter with an embarrassment of houses. The two homes were on opposite sides of William Street, 1920s-era with two stories and unfinished basements. She decided to sell one of them to us for a price my parents could just manage.

The only reason they had any money at all was that, just a week before the fire, Mom had been convinced by a travelling insurance salesman to buy a policy. A miracle. But even more amazing was the fact that the house we were buying was fully furnished, down to the knives and forks. The grand conflagration that Peter had created left us with nothing, so it was as if God reached down and touched my parents, saying, "Okay, you've had it a bit tough. Here you go: I'm going to cut you some slack." Of course this would mean you believed in God and not just good luck for a change.

There were beds and sheets and pillowcases. There were sofas and chairs and lights and, most amazing of all, a glorious solid-wood, hand-carved dining room suite complete with leather seats and a huge armoire. Even we kids who knew nothing knew this was something.

We moved in and spent the next eight years or so building memories of a dank, cold basement and a tiny little triangular bathroom. There were hardwood floors too, but in that day that was not very chi-chi, so Dad got a deal on some hardwearing Congoleum flooring that would withstand a nuclear attack. It was leftover from the new church and came very cheap—as in free. It was a very dark green with thin white swirls. In spite of all the hand-scrubbing and polishing it required it never looked clean, and after years of liquid wax it was always yellow around the edges. Every once in a while Mom would go on a cleaning binge and give one of us a sharp scraper and tell us to remove the yellow. It may be why not one of us ever became a dental hygienist.

The kitchen was too small and it became Mom and Dad's first renovation. Dad loved sledgehammers and knocked down walls with impunity. He designed and built new cupboards, extended the room and built a back porch. Then, as he did for every new project he undertook, he painted everything turquoise. It must have reminded him of warmer places. He said it was cheerful and bright. So we had turquoise cupboards and a turquoise porch. When he built bunk beds upstairs for us all to sleep in and huge drawers to hold our clothes he painted them turquoise too. The overall effect was like living in a robin's egg.

The only place Mom and Dad never touched was the basement. It was just too daunting. It had a low ceiling with huge beams that ran the length of the house. It had a damp concrete floor that was always seeping water around the edges. The washing machine was down there, too, surrounded by a mountain of dirty clothes. Some of those clothes never made it to the top of the pile; they just mouldered, getting more and more damp and dirty. Eventually, they would be unearthed like moles and thrown away. This is probably why we never had matching socks.

Mom avoided the basement. Who could blame her? Nothing good could come of her going down there. She had a wringer washer, the arm of which once flung up in protest at one too many loads of laundry and knocked out her front tooth. After that she became even more diligent in sending us down there to put the laundry on.

There were sacrifices to be made, though. None of us really cared about separating clothes, so all our socks were the colour of dirty snow. Things got shrunk and lost and that was just the way it was. The laundry was an insatiable monster that could not be appeased, so we stopped trying to satisfy it and did the minimum amount. Sometimes we wore things a little past their change-me date.

When the family fortunes improved and we moved away from this house, Mom bought a new machine called a mangler. I think that was a misnomer. When I think of mangling something I imagine it getting all wrung together, twisted and stretched beyond recognition. This machine did the opposite. It was a big, round, heated drum that had a lid that closed down. When you pulled the handle it sent jets of steam onto whatever was inside. My mom loved it. She ironed everything: hankies, Dad's boxer shorts, and tea towels. She liked flat things best. She did do the odd shirt and blouse but, really, they were an awful lot of work and not nearly so satisfying as a big pile of ironed face cloths.

In the William Street basement there were no manglers, but there were big wooden columns attached to some beams built around a furnace that looked like Shiva the many-armed Hindu god. Built into the walls three feet above the floor at either end of the basement were doors with old, rusty locks. Inside these doors was a long, low passageway with a damp, smelly dirt floor. We liked to play a game called "torture," which was just as it sounds: cruel and mean if you were the victim and great fun if you were the torturer. There were a series of tasks to be successfully completed. If you didn't complete them, more torture awaited.

The most frequent task required the person to go into the cupboard in the wall and crawl along on their hands and knees in the dark around the inside wall and emerge on the other side. The crawl of horror meant you were sure to feel things in the dark that could very well be dead mice or worse. You were absolutely guaranteed to have spider webs drift across your face and, worst of all, you weren't even sure if you were going in the right direction, because you had to do this in total darkness.

The best course of action was to scurry along on your hands and knees as fast as you could, holding your breath all the way if you were able. Then you banged really loudly on the door at the other end of the tunnel, demanding to be let out. Depending on the kindness of the person on the other side you might be let out right away or you might be made to wait while you threatened to pee your pants, scream really loudly, or kill them when you got out.

We also liked to tie people to the big beams, blindfold them and say we were going away. Then we would sneak back behind them and ever so gently stroke their neck with a rag, or just our fingertips. The more the person screamed the quieter we were. It all sounds evil and twisted now and I guess it was, but then it was just a little diversion.

There was also a kayak and an old sheepskin rug left hanging on a beam in the basement. They were the only reminders we had of the uncle who had enticed us to Canada. My mother and father had decided to come to Vancouver from England because my mom's brother was here and said it was the most beautiful place on Earth, clean and full of promise. A few months after we arrived in Canada he went back to England, never to return. I guess it wasn't that beautiful to him after all. But he left us that great old kayak, so it wasn't a complete loss. We would climb into the kayak, cover ourselves with the sheepskin and then rock back and forth. We told each other stories about being at sea in a big, high storm.

"Hang on," we yelled at each other. "Hang on, we're going over!"

It was an old, creaky house, this "mansion" on William Street, but it was ours and we were told many times how lucky we were to have it. I guess Peter didn't think so. He had been spectacularly successful in destroying our Mallairdville house. There was a gap of a few years before he thought he would try his hand at something exciting in our new house. Although he once again managed to create hardship and loss, this time the entire house didn't go up—it wasn't the stunning showstopper he was hoping for.

Not to be deterred, he gave it another shot in what may have been his most audacious plot yet. While we were all doing the get-ready-for-a-family-outing thing he hid and set another fire. It smouldered and burned the entire time we were away. The whole day we picnicked in the park he never let on that when we got home we would have a special surprise.

Like a very bad TV rerun, we returned to find piles of charred wood and debris yet again on the front lawn. We just assumed that someone had brought the junk from the backyard, which housed the remains of the last fire, into the front. Dad looked at it and swore in Croatian and said, "What a stupid thing to do. If I find out who did that...." Mom said, "I am not cleaning that up again"—not that she had cleaned it up in the first place. But it was the principle of the thing.

The neighbours ran out quickly and gleefully set us straight. These weren't remnants from the other fire. These were the remains of a new fire that had merrily blazed away while we were gone.

Things were getting seriously weird with our house bursting into flames without provocation. The really strange thing was that Mom and Dad never blamed Peter in front of us. Was it protection of him or pride? How do you admit your son is something quite strange, and probably evil, too? But his next fire fiasco left them no choice but to admit that maybe there was a problem here.

One evening he and his brain-trust chums decided that a really fun and clever thing to do would be to set fire to the tree in front of our house. They danced around it as it burned until someone came out and saw what was going on. Then while everyone was looking he ran straight into our house, just so there could be no doubt that he was involved. He got caught. His friends ran away, and Peter began his lifelong adherence to some bizarre version of *omertà*, that code of silence that all criminals think somehow elevates them to a nobler status—as if he were Italian or something. He took the whole rap.

Although burning down a tree wasn't that big a deal, even back then when crime seemed to have more of an impact on the forces that be, the whole thing went sideways. The burning tree on its own probably wouldn't have garnered more than a good beating from

Dad and several weeks of grounding, but this tree event combined with all of Peter's other misdemeanours got him some time in what they called "Juvi."

It almost sounds like fun, doesn't it? "Juvi," kind of short for jubilation? No, "Juvi" was juvenile hall. Even that has a sort of English boys' school sound to it. It was where Peter began to hone his criminal skills, became acquainted with some really bad guys and received confirmation that the world really was a horrible place where you hit before you got hit. He would make everyone pay.

The only one who paid was Peter. It was a good thing he was strong, since most of the time he was either beating someone up or getting the shit kicked out of him. That kind of ongoing abuse toughens you up and makes you ugly, too. You lose your teeth, your arms and legs get broken and of course you learn that food isn't nearly as entertaining as drugs. You become model-thin; although it's doubtful *Vogue* will come calling.

Peter learned to cook in prison. He was drawn to the creative aspect of it. I'm assuming it wasn't the knives. He mostly learned to bake cakes and pies. Pastry is fairly safe; it's hard to beat someone with a pie or suffocate them with a pastry shell.

Mostly, though, he embarrassed me. The day the story appeared in the paper outlining his latest job there was no end of kids willing to share it with me. Maybe a more mature person would have shrugged it off as his problem. But I was a nine-year-old who suffered such revelations badly. "Hey, your brother was in the paper. Wow, a bank robber!"

It was hard to deny the facts, since his name was in the paper. It was even spelled correctly (a rarity). But just what you would expect in this situation? He had decided that the best way to rob the bank would be to drive up with a truck with a ladder on top and ram the window with the ladder. Too bad it had the name and phone number of Dad's cleaning company on the side. He went to jail again.

My biggest gripe against him has always been the bugs. One day we found ourselves all covered in red, itchy bumps and blisters. Mom discovered he had brought home a really unwanted guest, in particular *Sarcoptes scabiei*—scabies. At this point in his wild life Peter, around sixteen years of age, was hanging out with some unsavoury types and doing more than just talking.

It seems scabies are very robust creatures. Like little miners they burrow under your skin, in the webs between your fingers and on your wrists and the backs of your elbows. And there they were on my groin and on my knees and on my poor little bum. Apparently men get them on their penis; I hope he had them there.

Mom told us that even though we were covered in hundreds of bumps and little blisters, there were probably not that many actual bugs; they were just leaving trails, like Boy Scouts blazing paths on our bodies. It's a wonder I have any skin left I scratched so much. The itch was insidious and relentless, especially at night, and I thought I would go crazy.

The upshot was that we had to stay home from school. Okay, that wasn't so bad. But while we were home we had to strip all the beds and boil the sheets and pillowcases in a big pot Mom had on the stove. It seemed that regular washing wasn't going to do it. We washed everything and slathered ourselves in some stinging lotion designed to kill the offending bugs.

I've since learned that the hot baths Mom made us take before applying the lotion are not such a good idea. The lotion is introduced into the blood stream through the skin, and in susceptible children it can cause seizures and even death. Well, wouldn't that have been the icing on the cake? They find us the next day, a mini Jones Town massacre, all the little bodies covered in something that was supposed to cure them. The paper would interview Mom (who would survive). "I didn't know; I thought it was the right thing to do," she would say stoically.

The whole "boil-everything-in-sight" approach was a terrible ordeal and almost more than Mom could bear. She was so worn out and I think embarrassed with the shame of this infestation that she could hardly muster any anger toward Peter. She needed all her strength just to deal with the fallout from our insect invasion. She did say through tight lips, "I know where you've been and now you are bringing that dirt into our house." If he was ashamed, I never heard about it.

At one point his activities got so bizarre that he convinced someone he was crazy. I already knew that. He was put into a mental hospital. It was built like a castle fortress and it had bars on the windows. They actually called it a clinic, which seems so clean and medicinal and helpful, but it wasn't.

Through all of this Mom and Dad swung between being confused at what they could not understand to fury to feeling hopeless enough to allow all kinds of well-meaning folks to convince them to fork over money they didn't have for "treatment" for Peter. He got counselling; they got counselling.

"He is acting out because he doesn't feel in control. You should give him more allowance." They did; it didn't help. I think one of those counsellors suggested that Peter didn't feel loved and wanted. "No, that can't be it," Mom and Dad said. "We love him. We treat him just like the rest of our children."

I was aware of events going on around me as a child as though I were looking into a big aquarium tank. Everything was a bit fuzzy and moving slowly. If a whale jumped out of the tank and splashed me, then I might notice.

The rest of us were just fed up. He was usually doing something he shouldn't be doing, like tying ropes from trees to gutters to test their strength. He was like a character in those Hardy Boys books, always looking for adventure, except Peter wasn't interested in learning how to tie new kinds of clever knots, set off on an adventure in a canoe or read animal tracks. Everything he got into was dangerous, involved damage and usually wound up with him receiving some kind of punishment.

Since we lived in such close quarters, Mom and Dad would eventually notice whatever Peter did. They would then demand to know who had done it. We couldn't tell on him, even though we really wanted to. Saving his skin resulted in us spending many nights in our rooms with no dinner. I never heard him say, "Hey, thanks for saving my butt, you guys." I think he just thought that is what we would always do. I'm not sure why we were all so focused on saving him. I suspect Helena had a lot to do with the unspoken Protect Pete rule. She was always so obedient, so good at school, so willing and able, and he wasn't. Somehow she thought she could save him. She still does.

Mom and Dad were working into the night trying to get Dad's maintenance company going. They cleaned office buildings and doctors' offices. All of this while Dad was still holding down his janitor job at Our Lady of Sorrows. They were trying to get their own company going so they could say "Bye bye" to that job of shame. They emptied garbage cans and washed out toilets and ashtrays. They vacuumed and they mopped. Then they got up the next day, Mom looked after us, Dad went to work at his school janitor job, and at night they did it all again.

Before taking on the job of janitor he had gone fishing in the summer with his Croatian contacts, painted bridges, wrapped heating pipes—he'd taken on any and all jobs that came his way. The job at Our Lady of Sorrows had come to Dad when we moved from Maillardville, scene of our burnt house, out to east Vancouver. He wanted to be his own boss and not have to listen to the whining sound of complaints from the nuns and priests. His pride is what kept him going—that and the fact he knew he could make more money on his own than he ever would in salary from the church. He and Mom were entrepreneurs without the Blackberries, trusty assistants, nice suits, power lunches or personal trainers.

I imagine that sometimes, alone in their bed at night, they must have made a plan. It may have been an unwritten pact in which they both signed on to do hard things every day. They would never say "No" to work. They would sacrifice themselves for us. Sacrifice is such an old-fashioned word and conjures up visions of martyrs, but I don't think they ever consciously thought about the sacrifices they were making. They just knew what had to be done.

Maybe somewhere down deep they wished they had chosen a different path, one less crowded with children. I never heard them say they were sorry they had so many kids. Once in a while one of us would say, "You shouldn't have had so many kids." Their response was always, "Okay, which ones shouldn't we have had?"

Objects in Mirror Are Closer than They Appear

There was an easy answer to that question. They shouldn't have had any of them except for me. I always wondered what it would have been like to be an only child. Imagine the pampering, the fuss they would have made over me. Imagine how they would have listened to me with their undivided attention. Imagine.

They often did say how proud they were to be the parents of such a large family. I don't think they were proud of us as people but rather of the fact that somehow they did it; they raised us all, fed us and clothed us and did it on their own. We were their career, their Mount Everest. They never talked about the cost to them. What would have been the point? We were there because of them. Like chickens with their farmers or sheep with their shepherds we were their responsibility.

In East Vancouver we were like those aliens you see in movies that look like everyone else but inside are very, very different. This was strange, really, because the neighbourhood was full of immigrants. I think our sheer numbers made us stand out from the crowd. We never really did fit in, and it was only our eventual move to the suburbs that would release us from the curse of being so different. But that move didn't happen for a long time, so there were lots of opportunities for us to make unspoken statements about our uniqueness. But we were kids. It was Mom and Dad who no doubt felt most keenly this sense of separateness. It must have been a tough job leading an army with dignity when the generals were also being assailed.

Maybe my parents were able to carry on raising twelve kids because they had their eye on some future reward. If they produced lots of snappy, clever little duffers who would some day become rich, highly paid professionals, we would gratefully look after them in their old age. Well, maybe, but I am surprised they would be so confident in that outcome given what could only be called our humble beginnings.

My own theory about why they had so many children flies in the face of what Mom always gave as their reason for so many kids. She cited religious duty or some variation on that theme as the driving force behind the big number. Now, after all these years, I think it was because my parents were here all alone in a country where they knew no one and no one knew or cared about them. Immigrants themselves—Mom from England and Dad from Croatia—they set about creating their own little community peopled with well-behaved children who did their bidding and understood them as much as anyone would or could.

They often left us alone with Helena, whose job it was to get us all into bed. Helena, the oldest and most responsible, was hyper-vigilant. She noticed everything. I guess that's what happens if you think you are responsible for everything. She organized, monitored and mothered us. Long before all those books were written on family dynamics and how placement decides your role, Helena was being the good one. She looked after all of us, but Peter has always been her really special job, her particular form of philanthropy. She protected him and played with him. She must have had x-ray vision to see something inside him worth saving. She still thinks there is, but many would question her belief. Helena has never been a churchgoing Catholic. She hasn't been a churchgoing anything. She does say, though, that she believes we are called to "love the sinner but not the sin."

She was brilliant just the way you would expect a first-born child to be. Current family birth-order theory states that the oldest child often has an IQ three to four points higher than their siblings. One of Helena's ex-husbands always maintained that most of us were not a very bright lot because we all had to have a share of brainpower and we each only got one twelfth.

At any rate, Helena knew how to keep us occupied and out of trouble. She and Peter made up stories. These adventures took us on ships, had us walking up mountains, camping alone and building campfires with no adults. They called this game, with a singular lack of originality, "Helena and Peter." Helena would call to him across the hall into the room where the boys slept. "Pe-e-ter," like a sweet singsong in three syllables. "He-le-e-na," he'd call back in response. And off we would go—free, innocent fun of which Helena was a master.

During that short time Peter seemed almost like an everyday kind of boy. But it didn't last. The next day he would get up and do some dumb-ass thing. I've always thought that maybe Peter was never quite right inside and that he couldn't be fixed. But when I remember those evening story sessions I wonder if he could have been saved. Maybe if he had been born into another family, if he had been an only child, the total focus of someone's attention and love.

The family has always been divided on Peter. One half thinks he is a no-good bum who steals from everyone, including his mother, and is beyond redemption. Others think he is a victim of circumstance; not properly or fully loved, with a mental condition that made him a drug addict. I'm not sure. But I am very curious about how and why someone chooses such an incredibly difficult life style when it really isn't working. I never thought I could help him, and really I didn't want to.

Helena, however, has always tried. She was always hopeful for him—without any good reason, really. In later years she would bail him out of jail; he would skip bail, taking her money with him. She paid to have him fly to some northern logging camp where he could cook and keep out of trouble. He stayed until he had enough money to come back. He is always drawn to those he feels most comfortable with. These are people who steal and lie and do even more drugs than he does. Among these folks he is the elder statesman. He has longevity on his side, along with a way of looking at the world that impresses those who have no view.

Peter is living to be what could be called an old man. In spite of what should have been several life-ending infections and diseases, he keeps on. This makes him feel guilty, and mad too. A kind of reverse "Why me?" I wonder if he thinks his longish life is his punishment.

∽

Kathleen O'Connell

You Are What You Eat

When our mom, the lovely Kathleen O'Connell, was little, her father called her "Titch." It meant small and pretty. It also implied a kind of helplessness. This was someone who needed to be picked up and carried, fussed over, coddled and protected. She loved it.

As a young woman she was stunningly beautiful. In a picture taken when she was eighteen she looked so soft and luscious and lush. Her thick wavy hair was elegantly arranged and she had a hopeful, sweet smile on her perfect Cupid's bow mouth. The boys were crazy about her. She was "it," and smart too. She won a scholarship to a good private finishing school where she took elocution lessons and excelled in math. But Kathleen wasn't relying on her brains to get her ahead. She knew that a beautiful face and a curvy figure were her ticket out of town.

Her father was gassed in the war. It made his lungs and spirit weak. He never really worked after that. He called himself a cobbler, but mostly he just fixed his own family's shoes. He adored my mom, and she always kept buried deep a memory of that love and time in her life when she was truly special and treasured. Most of her life was spent remembering that she was once someone's little girl and wondering what went wrong.

Her mother went off and cleaned houses while Mom's brothers decided their role in life was to drink a lot. Mom's eldest sister, Eileen, was the strong, capable one. Even though she was older than my mom, somehow she ended up doing her sister's bidding. When Dad first started courting Mom, Eileen had to bring them refreshments as if she were the maid. Eileen never forgot that humiliation, and I doubt if Mom ever remembered it. She probably would have seen it as her due.

Domestic duties were not Mom's responsibility. She never learned to cook. She claimed it was because her mother wouldn't let in her in the kitchen. When she married Dad at eighteen she knew how to make porridge. He was appalled. He tried to show her how it went. He introduced her to spices beyond salt and pepper. She tried, but it was like teaching a parrot to speak—it sounds like words but the meaning just doesn't come through. She always blamed her bad cooking on the sheer number of us, as if she was cooking for hundreds every night. She implied that if she could just create an intimate dinner for four we would be so impressed and she would win cooking awards.

She got a lot of support for her theory. "Oh, your poor mom. How does she do it? Of course she just cooks basic food." The implication was that it was nutritious and delicious if not fancy. It's true none of us died of scurvy or beriberi.

She developed and passed on to us a few basic recipes that involved big pots of things bubbling away on the stove. There was a soup Dad taught her to make. It contained purple beans, vinegar and a ham hock. I'd like to say how much of each but, apparently, there wasn't a recipe. Any recipe involving vinegar and ham should be approached cautiously, and Mom wasn't cautious. Maybe she didn't care how it or anything she cooked turned out, because by the time she sat down to eat there was either very little left, it was cold or she didn't want it. She would have been happy eating nothing but bread and potatoes. But not rice.

"Rice is lazy man's food," she declared. What she meant was you just put it in the pot with water and it cooked and it didn't involve hours of peeling, cutting, boiling and mashing. Rice wasn't real food.

Fine for her to praise the potato. She didn't have to go with the big pan down to the damp, dark basement into the cupboard under the stairs where the potatoes lived. Mom bought her potatoes in forty-pound burlap sacks from the potato man. You could smell them before you saw them. They sat quietly in that sack and patiently grew eyes. Soft and softer they grew, just waiting, biding their time until you reached in and touched them, shrieked and pulled back. Now you had to gather the courage to reach in again. You could always pull the eyes off but you couldn't come back empty-handed. We were hunter/gatherers in search of the elusive firm potato. Mom would not be denied her potatoes no matter the psychic damage done to her children as they retrieved them.

But it was canned goods that really formed the staple of our diet. There was a store in a rundown part of town that sold bent and dented cans of food. It was a fun challenge to root through those bins to find the huge cans of beans with the greasy but highly valued piece of pork, spaghetti in tomato sauce, stewed tomatoes, canned peas and the highly coveted but rarely bought Chef Boyardee mini ravioli. It was years before I knew that peas were green and that spaghetti was actually hard and didn't come round and solid, in the shape of a can, held together with red sauce. Cans without labels were even cheaper. Inside these mystery cans were often treats like apricots in syrup or fruit cocktail with the two maraschino cherry halves. Sometimes you weren't so lucky and ended up with artichoke hearts or water chestnuts or those little baby corns. Mom didn't know what to do with any of them, so the dog usually got an exotic feast.

Mom triumphed at meals based on several opened cans that were cleverly combined in a pot. These cans were the first step in her culinary evolution from creating time-consuming crappy meals to "heat-and-serve" crappy meals.

Forget putting a man on the moon or discovering semiconductors. In my mother's opinion it was the creation of instant food that was really moving mankind ahead. Anything that said, "Just add water" was an invention worth getting excited about. Her favourite was potato flakes. They were the best of all worlds: a foodstuff that looked just like potatoes and didn't need peeling. Even though she never peeled a potato, there was something so wonderful about any food that practically cooked itself.

There was a dessert called Jell-O One, Two, Three. It was magic. You whipped it up, and through some strange alchemy it made itself into three layers of pastel-coloured chemicals. You could top it with our other favourite dessert, Whip and Chill, a little cap of soft, snow-white Cool Whip. Jell-O was the original just-add-water dessert and perfect in its simplicity. I will always be grateful that Mom never tried to do as they suggested in the Kraft commercials: just add marshmallows, a little mayonnaise and a few shredded carrots. She felt that was really too much like cooking.

The real mystery, though, was how you went from thinking that cooking was stirring something out of a package into hot water to serving your family stuffed cow's heart. It sounds like something Caligula would serve up to an enemy. It looked just like a human heart but larger and thicker. It even had those tubes leading out from it just in case you forgot it was once attached to something alive. There was a tracery of veins just under the surface and a thin, clear membrane of connective tissue that no amount of cooking would destroy. And Mom cooked it until it was black on the outside, like something tied to a stake. The stuffing inside the heart was really beside the point. The heart was the star of the show.

"Organ meat is full of iron," my mother said defensively. As if she cared about iron. Cow heart was cheap. She knew it and we knew it. We didn't care if eating it would make us live forever. It was still a heart. Who eats hearts? The sad truth was that we did. And before we left the table we always said, "Thank you for dinner, Mom."

Dad's cooking was different, too, but in an ethnically interesting sort of way. Today every restaurant worth its chops serves calamari, but when we were kids no one except maybe immigrants were eating squid. It was special-occasion food that Dad ordered well in advance and bought in big frozen blocks. He must have really loved it, because, as much as Mom loved the non-cook variety of meal, his cooking, especially the squid, was extremely labour-intensive. He spent so much time with them he could have named them.

First, he had to defrost those greyish blocks of ice, which took at least two days. Sometimes he forgot this step and was forced to return the squid to a cold, watery home in our bathtub to make them defrost more quickly. Once they were unfrozen they looked like alien beings with their pointy-heads, tubular bodies and those long, wiggly tentacles. Now he had to split open their still-icy bodies and scoop out the soft goo inside, and since some of these squid were going to be mothers you had to remove the eggs as well. Finally, he cut each squid into bite-sized pieces. It's hard to believe now that we could even want to eat those strange chunks. I am sure that if we had been called upon to have as much to do with those squid as Dad did we never would have eaten them.

The now-unrecognizable-as-squid pieces were dredged in seasoned flour and deep-fried. We fought over the crispy tentacles, which were strangely sweet and salty and oh so crunchy. I think the secret ingredient may have been the deep fryer. It was filled with fat that had been used so many times to cook so many things it was a deep brown. The pot that held that fat was practically a member of the family. It had a thick, black crust on the outside that would have taken a jackhammer to remove, and a wire basket the same colour as the oil.

"Why throw away perfectly good oil we've only fried potatoes and a few fish sticks in?" Mom was the original recycler. So what if the stuff looked like the tar sands? She even tried to tell us it was full of nutrients from all the past food that had been in it. We didn't buy it and we didn't care. None of us was concerned about trans fats or our cholesterol levels. We never told anyone we were eating squid—we didn't need one more reason to be singled out as weird and different—but apple strudel? Now, that was something different.

Normally a pastry chef is a member of the classic *brigade de cuisine*, a whole army of people dedicated to creating something truly memorable. Dad was the entire brigade. He prepared, he assembled, and he patted and touched and waited. To watch him create apple strudel was to see him in a different, almost altered, state: calm, relaxed and utterly focused.

He started with a small piece of pastry no bigger than a baseball. He covered the dining room table with a white tablecloth, dusted it with flour and rolled the dough into a pie-sized circle. Then he put his hands under the tablecloth and pulled and stretched and pulled that dough until it was translucent and almost as large as the table. Onto this thin sheet he shaved apple slices, raisins, brown sugar and rum. We stared as he rolled up the dough into a long, long roll. We all sent up a silent prayer: "Oh God, don't let it tear or break." We could imagine the cursing, the shouting, and the high drama that would surround a ruined strudel. We watched as he curled the now-fat roll of pastry around the special pan head to tail, slit the top, sprinkled it with water, dusted it with sugar and baked it. Heaven was that flaky, juicy, apple-filled strudel. Throughout this entire event he rarely spoke and worked with an intensity that created a zone of magical quiet all around him. He seemed so happy to be doing something so creative, something beautiful for his family, something he could be proud of.

∼

Pauline & Dad

What Doesn't Kill You...

You would think that losing her eye would be enough pain, suffering and trauma in Anita's life. But no one ever said life is fair, so she was one more time the unlucky bystander when Peter screwed up.

It was a day much like another and Dad was furious at Peter again, probably because Peter's entire role in life seemed to be to infuriate Dad. Everything about him was annoying and he knew it. We all knew that the paintbrush Dad threw wasn't supposed to hit Anita. It was aimed at Peter. But he was a wily, quick and slippery guy. He ducked, Anita didn't, and it caught her on that thin-skinned, bony place just above the eye, above what we now called her "good eye," like her other eye was somehow to blame for not being there. It bled like cuts on your head love to do. Dad saw the blood and swore. Mom came in, saw the blood and said nothing. She grabbed Anita and a dirty tea towel and pressed it firmly to her head. It continued to bleed.

At this point Anita should have been on her way to the hospital to have a stitch or two. She wasn't. Instead she was sitting on a chair in the kitchen holding that tea towel tightly to her head and crying quietly. She didn't want to make Dad madder. She was again in the wrong place at the wrong time.

But Anita was more than just a glass eye. Much to Mom's disappointment and surprise Anita also had large, luscious breasts, just like Mom did when she was young. And because all straight guys basically want those breasts, Anita was very popular in her teens. Amazingly she dyed her hair blonde early and, combined with her strong, fit body, she had all she needed to attract those trembling boys. Mom couldn't help but diminish and belittle Anita's obvious charms. Mom didn't feel any conscious or unconscious jealousy toward me. I had no breasts and the boys avoided me.

In spite of the fact that Anita and I were as different as chalk and cheese we were, as they used to say, pals. I trusted her and she tolerated me. We were both girls, eighteen months apart, but beyond that we were really the yin and yang of teenagehood. Anita was remarkably confident and I was a crouching, grouching insecure tag-along. They say you get what you deserve, but I didn't deserve Anita or her unstinting forgiveness. If she thought unkind things about me she never said them aloud. If she wished I would just "grow up" and stop clinging to her, she didn't say that either.

Anita and I would go to high school dances where, just like every other excruciatingly anxious teenage girl, I wanted to be "chosen." It didn't happen. Anita, however, was highly successful at this game, and she generously gave me lessons on where to stand out at the front of the pack of teenagers circling the dance floor. Her advice was simple and to the point: "Smile. Guys come over if you smile." It seemed such a simple formula, but I knew it had more to do with what was going on inside my head than any smile I could force on my face.

It didn't help that I chose to sit on the benches at the back of the gym. I knew this was not the way to attract anything but all the other sad, disappointed girls. But there was something so desperately unfair in the whole thing. Why did I have to wait for some pimply-faced guy to choose me so I could jerk around the floor with him, not making eye contact? I had put all the effort into preparing myself. They should be lined up begging me to dance with them.

I had lovingly laid my empty dress out on the bed with the blue fishnet nylons tucked underneath to get the full effect. It looked like a very flat version of me. I sat and looked at it, thinking it looked better without me in it. Then there was my hair. Long, straight, smooth hair was what everyone wanted, and it seemed everyone, including Anita, had it. I had short, brown nonconformist hair that looked ridiculous, like a curly clown wig. But I had a system for taming my hair, perfected through practise.

First I had Helena cut it very short to avoid the most obvious curls. Then I smoothed big blobs of Dippity-do gel through my hair. That gelatinous goo was the saviour of many a teenage girl's curly hair. I followed this application with surgically applied rolls of transparent tape. All of this was to achieve the pixie/gamin look that was the only acceptable alternative to long and straight. If I did it just right there wouldn't be any telltale ridges between the strips after I peeled them off. This was a time-consuming, tricky process. If I used too much gel it would flake off and look like scaly, dead skin.

My hair felt quite apart and separate from me as it sat atop my head, an evil creature that gave me no peace. I never really won the daily battles I fought with it throughout my adolescence. Cutting and taping my hair had come after I had tried many times to flatten it with an iron. I laid my head down on the ironing board and spread my hair out. Then I tried to get the iron as close to the top of my head as possible. There is a special smell to burning hair that signals it's time to remove the iron. If you didn't want to burn your scalp—and let's face it, who does—you will have left a little indentation. If you looked at the top of my head and followed it down a few inches, there'd be the telltale ironing ridge, then more hair in various stages of straightness. Not quite the look I was after and, overall, a little sad. My attempt at being cool ended up like most of my early fashion forays—badly.

As we walked home from these failed dances, me with my semi-straightened or taped short hair, I blamed Anita for my lack of success. "Maybe if you'd stick around me a bit instead of going off and leaving me so you could flirt with those guys. Mom said you were supposed to stay with me."

I groused and complained and swore I'd never go again. She knew I was lying. The truth was I wanted and needed to feel just once that gentle nudge of joy at being asked to dance, of being accepted at a high school dance. I'd seen the happy glow of satisfaction on the faces of other girls as they were asked and swept off onto the dance floor. And I always thought, "Next time; it will be my turn next time." I knew that some day I would get all the fashion pieces in order, I would affect just the right smile and give off a wild scent of confidence and, finally, I would receive the attention I deserved. And, anyway, I had two eyes.

∼

Pauline, Anita, Mom, Eileen, Helena and "The Car"

Poor is a Four-letter Word

Some people have found ways to deal with their humble beginnings. They glamorize them or turn them into an object lesson. They talk about the resiliency they build, the strength of character, the ability to deal with challenges and misfortune and keep on smiling as you climb the ladder of success—the Little Orphan Annie approach to life. There's a huge section in most bookstores devoted to just such a tack. They have titles like "I Did and So Can You," "You Are What You Say You Are," "Letting Go of the Past: Embracing Your Future."

When I was a kid we were just poor. It was part of who we were, like being immigrants and having a father who spoke with an accent that no one but we could understand.

We weren't Irish-potato-famine poor, or eating-dirt poor (although some of us did this by choice), or running-around-with-bare-feet-in-winter or smelling-like-you-didn't-have-running-water poor. We were just the kind of poor that describes your current situation and hints at your future possibilities. The kind of poor that makes it probable you will be given the second-hand coat of a girl in your school when you have a house fire that burns all your coats. That girl will sing in the choir with you and she will tell everyone who will listen that the coat you're now wearing, that one right there—it was hers. We were that kind of poor.

Then Mom and Dad discovered camping and decided this was the perfect vacation for us. It fulfilled the number-one requirement: it was cheap. We could do it together and we could get away from home. What more could you ask?

Our camping vacations were our first tentative forays into the world of the middle class. But just in case we started to get too uppity, events came along to remind us of just who we were, what we could expect and what could happen to those who got too big for their britches.

When we went camping we packed all our worldly goods in pillowcases. This had two advantages: you can get a lot in a pillowcase, and you can put your tightly packed pillowcases in a too-small car and the kids can sit on them. There were pillowcases for the little kids and the big kids, Mom and Dad had a suitcase, and there were communal pillowcases for things like shoes, boots and swimsuits. It was all very sensible and creative of our parents. They had it down to a fine art and could have given seminars on packing in smart and efficient ways. Of course you would have to be willing to wear clothes so wrinkly they looked like Shar Pei puppies.

One year, like every year, the chaos of stuffing the car began; after lots of crying, swearing in Croatian, threats of cancelling the whole thing and general mayhem and confusion we set off. It wasn't until we arrived at our campsite and were vibrating with anticipation of the first swim that the horror became clear. The pillowcase with the swimsuits was still sitting by the door.

This is where being poor comes in. Forget the car or home or job as arbiters of wealth; it is the swimsuit that made it clear who we were and what we could expect. It was a coveted luxury item, like whole milk or chicken cacciatore with real meat instead of chicken necks and backs. If you had money you might still go and buy new bathing suits. When you are poor this is not going to happen. They were not necessary for survival.

If my mother hadn't married at eighteen and proceeded to have children for most of her adult life, I think she could have run the world. She was mentally agile and able to imagine low-cost solutions. Today a mind like hers would earn a spot as a CEO for a big multinational. She knew where to find efficiencies, she thought "outside the box" and she was ruthless and unyielding.

Our mother and father both lived in another world of decision-making, into which we were not invited. They made secret, often painful decisions we were privy to only after they were made. The swimsuits were a prime example. To Mom, the solution was simple. She would buy inexpensive little boy swimming trunks, the older boys could wear their shorts, and the baby girls and boys could wear a t-shirt and a diaper. But what were adolescent girls expected to do?

Mom found it hard to summon sympathy for teen or pre-teen girls. As a stunning young woman she had had a clutch of boys who doted on her. She loved and came to expect that kind of attention. And then she married and lost her drawing power. But there was still a voice inside her that said, "You're beautiful and deserve to be admired and spoiled."

This dream vision ran contrary to her current circumstances. She looked around at her daughters who were moving into a place where that kind of attention could conceivably be theirs. She loved us, but she wasn't going to do anything that drew positive attention to us or our developing bodies. Or maybe she was just being cheap.

On her trip to the small town for boy suits, Mom bought little bras, tiny white triangles with straps and two eyes and hooks for our triple-A breasts and some thin, blue-flowered material. By the light of the campfire she sewed covers on those little bra tops and cut out and sewed us matching shorts, with neat little hems, finished off with elastic-band waists. They screamed homemade—bad homemade, living-in-the-country-milking-cows homemade, we-will-never-be-cool-no-one-will-ever-like-us homemade. I refused to wear mine.

"Fine," said my mother in a flat, monotone voice. "Then you're not going swimming."

I waited for the rant or the threats. They didn't come. My mother was the queen of unspoken guilt. She telegraphed it with her stance and her look. She didn't need to say what was clearly on her mind. "Fine. I sat by that fire ruining my eyes sewing you a swimsuit and this is how you thank me."

And still, standing by the edge of the lake, my back burning, head sweating, I refused to wear it. A weird suntan from t-shirts and shorts developed and I refused to wear the suit. I never wore it.

Anita wore hers. She wasn't able to withstand the glares of guilt. I was made of sterner stuff. My anger sustained me. Sitting by the edge of the lake chewing my nails, I thought of how stupid my mother was. Who asked her to sit by a campfire in the dark and sew those ugly swimsuits with tiny little stitches? Even here by the lake, where we could have pretended we were just like everyone else, she had to make swimsuits that screamed "No Money Here!"

We were away from Our Lady of Sorrows parish where we were the family that was an object of pity with all those kids. We could have left that all behind. But even here she wanted to make it clear we were poor. "We'll show you before you tell us." And it wasn't enough to admit we were poor—she wanted us to be poor and proud. In her world of hand-stitched bathing suits she found some kind of dignity. Lucky her.

∼

Pauline and Anita

This Way Home

As Dad's business improved so did our finances—enough, in fact, that we could move from our William Street home to a new modern home in the suburbs. When Mom and Dad took us to look at it I wasn't prepared for the splendour. It had two bathrooms with burgundy toilets and bathtubs. It was huge, with five bedrooms, a rec room complete with wood panelling and a built-in bar covered with studded leatherette. It had a big window in the front room that looked out onto a long, wide green front lawn. The younger kids liked it but the older crowd, myself included, were thrilled. "We've arrived!"

Here was space. Yes, there were still too many kids around, but living here in the suburbs with all the other everyday folk made me feel as if we were now part of the mainstream. Away from the eastside neighbourhood with all its immigrants, we could begin a new, more prosperous life, a life where we could blend in and become part of the regular world. This regular world was where people didn't spend all their time thinking about money. They weren't always worried about where to get it and how to spend the least amount you could. We were delirious when we left our house on the eastside; it meant a new beginning in a new part of town, a place where nobody really knew us. We could start fresh and create our own story.

In the initial relative vacuum, without any information and before folks came to understand we were just a very large family, myths about us floated around our new suburban neighbourhood. The local fire department had gathered together coats and clothes to bring over to Mom because they thought she and Dad were running an orphanage.

The move to the suburbs coincided with my final year at Our Lady of Sorrows. It had been a very long eight years, but I was finally free. In honour of the move the decision was made that Anita and I would go to a public school. This was going to be my chance to really spread my wings and become the person I knew I could be. I'd be smart and popular, the one everyone wanted for a friend. I would let my hair grow and I would become sophisticated. The real Pauline was finally going to shine through.

What I found is that there are some ways of being that are bone-deep. When all you have ever known is the gulag of a Catholic school, it's hard to let it go. There I was in my new public school, leaping to my feet when the teacher came in the room just as I had always done for the nuns, wearing matching sweater sets and barrettes in my hair because I didn't have a clue about how to dress if it wasn't a uniform. Something about me really pissed off those public school boys. Besides dressing like a nerd, I'm pretty sure I spoke in a way that sounded stuck up, stupid and judgmental. After all, I knew nothing, and the last resort of the uninformed is to be as bombastic as possible. Get them before they get you and all that.

One day I must have really gone too far. One of the guys came up to me and, with his face so close to mine I could smell his spearmint gum and see the acne medication caked on his zits, whispered, "The best part of you ran down your mother's leg." I had no idea what that meant. But I knew it was something bad because of his low and slow delivery and the fact that everyone stared at him and then at me and then huddled together and walked quickly away.

At Our Lady of Sorrows, finking on other kids was considered normal and natural and was even encouraged. I hadn't had many chances to tell on other kids—I was usually the one that got told on. But I knew how it went. You worked yourself up into a frenzy of tears and anger and then stormed off and told the nun, and suitable punishment was delivered to the offending party.

So that's what I did. I marched right up to the teacher that day and repeated word for word what that boy had said to me. The teacher stared at me in disbelief. He blinked. He opened his mouth. He closed his mouth. He blinked again. There must have been for him a complete disconnect. How did those words come out of the mouth of such a dorky kid? I was feeling so self-righteous and proud. I had stood up for myself.

Finally, he said, "Yes, well, yes. I'll, I'll certainly be speaking to him."

I can imagine the scene in the staff room when he reported that one. I don't know if he ever did speak to that kid and I didn't really care. I was just sick of putting up with the old bullshit. I smiled all the way home and of course told no one about it. It was my own secret, private victory. That's how messed up I was. I actually thought I had won.

What I didn't know was that as I was recounting my tale of woe that boy and his buddies were standing just outside the classroom door. They heard my whole whining disclosure, and that single act of independence sealed my fate. I was thereafter a pariah and avoided at all costs. There are no pictures of me from that year at public school. It's as if it didn't happen. As if.

I begged to be able to go back to Catholic school. I wanted to return to the well-remembered aches and pains and the familiar craziness. I knew my place in that Catholic-school world. In a Catholic high school there wouldn't be any ugly surprises.

Anita, on the other hand, would have been very happy to stay. She'd found her place in the bigger realm of public high school. They had PE classes and a running club and she was a good runner. She'd made friends and was popular. But there was no way Mom and Dad would let her stay there having fun while I was off at St. Patrick's by myself. I probably made a fuss and demanded that she come with me. Unfortunately for Anita, my bitching, combined with Mom's campaign to keep her in her place, meant she had to go too.

After my one-year failed attempt at public school, I had given up my dream of being a normal teenager and settled for the familiar. Rather than the daily confusion and missteps that took place in a regular high school, I returned to the safe, warm bosom of a Catholic high school.

It was an hour-and-a-half bus ride there and back. Rich private schools had their own bus where you didn't have to mix with the rest of the world; we travelled with the plebeians on the "loser cruiser" of public transit and tried not to get noticed—not easy when you are wearing navy and white uniforms, knee-high socks, black and white saddle shoes and a blazer.

We had a very peculiar little tie that was actually a strip of ribbon folded over with a buttonhole in it. You attached this tie to the top button of your blouse. The effect, of course, was to ensure that at all times your blouse was buttoned right up to the neck. We never wore this tie on the bus and undid our blouses as far as we could, which wasn't very far. I had normal-size feet, but in those saddle shoes they looked like they belonged to a very big man. I tried to tuck them under the bus seat, but then I would forget and they would slip out, threatening to trip anyone who came within six inches.

There was a slightly old-fashioned air to the whole getup, which we tried to mitigate by hiking our uniforms up to miniskirt length once we were around the corner from home. There were little woollen tams, too, but there was no way to wear them without looking like young French hookers. All around a very bad look for two teenage girls.

Saint Patrick's was like Our Lady of Sorrows in the way Froot Loops are like porridge. Both are breakfast cereals but one is just so much more interesting. The first and most helpful thing about St. Pat's was that Dad was not the custodian or our gym teacher. By now Dad's carpet-cleaning and maintenance business was doing very well and we were almost respectable. It is okay to have twelve children as long as you have money and can contribute to the running of the school and church.

Now we were just part of the crowd of mostly immigrant Catholic kids hanging out together. Italians, Irish, Filipino, Greek—we had a shared understanding of the Catholic doctrine but didn't believe a word of it. The endless praying was modified, although we did still take a daily class called religious studies. These were the classes where people were gently encouraged to consider the religious life. We were shown the glory of dedicating our lives to God, the intense joy from spending longs hours in prayer and sacrifice and, on the practical side, receiving a paid education. I would rather have stuck a hot needle in my eye.

Anita, on the other hand, did consider it. The nuns were ecstatic, and for a while she was treated like royalty as befits a future Bride of Christ. When she changed her mind all her specialness disappeared in a vapour of disappointment. Then the nuns treated Anita with the kind of disdain reserved for spurned lovers.

Our religious lessons were also opportunities for the priest to come over and give us his version of sex education. He seemed most concerned about masturbation. He spoke about it often and usually in metaphors. My favourite was the masturbation-as-a-train-engine theory. The way he explained it, masturbating was like starting up a train engine and warming it up over and over again and then shutting it down just before it got going "with a full head of steam." It seems that if you do this too often, when you want the engine to really get going it won't, because of all the false starts. He suggested we just leave the train in the engine yard until we really needed it (read, get married) and then rev that puppy up and let 'er go.

For me, discovering masturbation was a wonderful, terrifying surprise—a gift from my vagina to me. Of course we didn't call it a vagina. In my family we called it our "tuppeny" from the word tuppence or two pennies. Made sense to us. The penis was called a John Willie. I don't know why.

No one told my parents about the importance of giving children the real name for their body parts. They didn't seem to understand that without the proper names we wouldn't be able to carry on as functional human beings. Well, they may have been strange names, but they were our names. (We also called poo "bigs," as in "He did bigs in his pants." There was a family in our school whose last name was Biggs. Laugh—we thought we'd cry.)

I started masturbating young and vigorously. It seemed harmless until I found out much later in the usual ways that this feeling was connected to something bigger—something Catholic girls are not supposed to know anything about or, more importantly, do anything about.

I remember the shock when one day I found out that my parents must have been doing that nasty thing. A kid at high school had said, "Wow, your mom and dad must fuck all the time." I was horrified and told her to shut up; she didn't know anything. As I was walking home it slowly filtered through and I realized it must be true. All that talk about men and women and "doing it"—that was my mother and father. It left me feeling quite sick. Over time, however, I developed a strange pride in them. They knew what they were doing and they did it often. I think I also was dimly aware that if they could do it then, Goddamn it, some day so could I.

Besides religious lessons we also suffered through the same classes as kids in public schools. We had the same range of strange types that seemed to get a calling to teach, except of course at St. Pat's there was a mixture of "lay" people—anyone not of a religious order—and the nuns. It was a particularly potent blend of social misfits and zealots. You had to wonder why anyone would want to teach there if you could teach in a "real" high school. Probably most weren't really teachers, just people who showed up. They did have to be Catholic, though. That has got to be why they gave a job to our extremely myopic PE teacher.

I overstate it to say he taught PE. He taught basketball, and you had better like basketball because there was nothing else. My father's PE lessons were models of educational innovation compared to his. Looking back on it, that guy had the job most guys would want. He sat around all day watching kids play basketball through his bottle-glass lenses. Well, some kids played basketball. Mostly we sat with him on the benches watching the kids who already knew how to play. Remarkably, they won games sometimes, and I guess that's why he kept his job.

I tried out for the team, even though playing basketball was for me only slightly more fun than being at the dentist's office. He was very egalitarian. If you came to practise you played. Of course if you were me, you played in the last two minutes when we were either so far ahead or losing so badly that how you played didn't matter.

I only did it for one year, and then I discovered something lots more fun and very cool: smoking. Smoking became my time-consuming hobby. I spent most of my after-school time down at the local restaurant smoking while sharing a Coke with three other girls who had also discovered the amazing effects of a cigarette on your self-esteem. I loved smoking. I loved the whole business of lighting, sucking in deep breaths, blowing it out through your nose and mouth and staring in a world-wise way at the lighted tip of your cigarette, as though the secrets to the universe could be found there. There was nothing about it I didn't love. I held that cigarette in my hand and became clever and sophisticated. I became a person you would definitely want to meet and spend a wonderfully witty afternoon with.

My favourite place to smoke around the school was the meditation/prayer room. Toward the end of religious class was the best time to seek permission.

"Sister, may I be alone and pray on everything I heard today?" I would say in the sincerest tone I could manage. Off I would go to spend a little quality time with my Players cigarettes. It was a small room under the stairs. It had a table and a few wooden chairs and pictures of the saints cut out from religious calendars. It was remarkably well sealed, so the smoke didn't seem to drift out. I had usually prearranged for someone else to meet me there. We felt brave and carefree. While we were smoking we would put out little crumbs for the mice that also prayed there.

If we really felt the need to break free, the other option was to go into the library, push out one of the big, hinged windows, drop down to the grass below and run like hell to the cafe around the corner. Oh, the delirious relief. To be out in the middle of the day smoking a cigarette was nirvana. It couldn't get any cooler than that. The real miracle is that we never got caught. I always marvelled over that: how could that be—didn't they notice, didn't they care? I think we were just lucky and a little bit careful. We usually made it back by the end of the "study session" we had escaped from. Those little escapades were the nearest we ever came to the whole myth about private schools as places of zany, good-natured fun and adventure, places where the privileged few engaged in harmless pranks and everyone had a wonderful time.

Compared to Our Lady of Sorrows and my one foray into public school, my first few years at St. Pat's were a picnic. I felt slightly more in control. After all, it had been my idea to go there and I had a group of friends as weird and unfocussed as me. Life was good.

It was a mistake to think that way, I knew. The minute you let your guard down terrible things can happen.

There were two ways of being at St. Pat's. You could be bound for university or you could go into what they euphemistically called "commerce." It was for everyone who wasn't going to university, the dummies, those who didn't quite measure up. In Grade 9 and 10 I was in the university stream, but by Grade 11 I had shown my true colours and it was clear my future lay elsewhere.

The nun called my parents and I in to "discuss my future." Remember I'm fifteen. For me the future means tomorrow or maybe the weekend; beyond that was just a grey mist. Clearly, this nun had a long-range vision of me and it didn't look good.

In the most sympathetic of voices she said, "Now, Mr. and Mrs. Gojević," hands on her desk forming a little tent, "some children are just not made to go to university."

It was pretty clear which children she was talking about. She looked at my parents with an expression I think was supposed to imply understanding and deep care. She looked like she was holding back a fart. She pursed her lips and stared at us with watery blue eyes behind her black-rimmed glasses.

"God has other plans for them," she continued in her most carefully modulated voice, as if I weren't there.

I was pretty sure that God's plans didn't include anything fun or glamorous for me, like fashion photography or deep-sea diving.

"Pauline would do well to learn to type and take shorthand. In this way she could become a useful, contributing member of society."

Then she delivered what I guess she thought was her *coup de grâce*.

"I know you only want the best for her."

Ha. She must have thought they had huge plans for me and she was dashing their hopes for my glittering future. I got the feeling that, long ago, my parents had come to grips with the fact I wasn't going to be bringing home prizes. We had never had and never did have the what-do-you-want-to-be-when-you-grow-up conversation. Their attention to all of us took a very strange form. Around the home they were like circling hawks. They knew where we were every minute. Brief times away from the house were always preceded by many questions about where we were going, who we would be with and to the minute the time we needed to be back. The family unit was tight, like a noose.

When it came to our futures, however, academic or otherwise, they were blind, deaf and mute. Maybe they couldn't imagine a future for us. Maybe they just thought it would all play itself out in some mysterious way. I never saw them as fatalists but they sure behaved that way. Maybe they just thought we were damn lucky to be here moving forward in any way and that should be enough.

So, they agreed with her and I spent Grade 11 learning to type and do shorthand, easy math—I liked that part—and a very strange, watered-down version of English literature. What would a secretary need with any facility for English?

That year in commerce was wasted except for typing. Our typing teacher was a woman with short, stiff red hair that stuck out all over. Her eyes, which never blinked, were lashless and a startling blue. She wore sensible, laced-up brown shoes and matching jackets and calf-length skirts in a variety of plaid patterns. She had been a gunner in the Second World War and loud noises or sudden movements easily spooked her, so it was strange that she was stuck all day in the typing room with the cacophony of the typewriter keys and slamming carriages. During class she walked up and down correcting posture, readjusting fingers and hands and calling out a steady stream of instructions.

"Sit up straight, feet on floor, eyes on paper, do not look at your fingers." Over and over she said it like a mantra. It was calming and instructive.

The best thing about her was that she didn't seem to know or want to know who any of us were. This neglect was just what I was looking for. I was so tired of the unwanted, soul-destroying attention

I received from the nuns. They berated and belittled, found fault and revelled in public displays of mortification. This woman by contrast treated us all the same. If we made mistakes she talked about the mistake and didn't manage to bring up all the times you had made mistakes in the past and the mistakes your brothers and sisters had made and the mistakes you were going to make in the future.

Poor lady; she didn't make it through the year. They said she had a nervous breakdown. That seemed so unfair, but I started to understand that things are not as they appear. It was starting to become clear that the world worked for some and not for others. The really scary part, though, was the realization that terrible things happened to older people, too, and that just getting older was no guarantee of any respite from bad luck.

Anita was also in commerce. (Apparently Gojevićs were not university material. How could we be? Our dad ran a cleaning business. We were immigrants. We hadn't paid our dues yet.) She graduated from commerce actually having learned things, but for me one year of shorthand and typing and no expectations from anyone triggered something. I decided I was not going to sit at a desk all day. At least that is what I told everyone.

The real reason was I was just as bad at shorthand as I was at math. I knew I would never get a job taking dictation and I really didn't want to. I had no idea what I would do at university, but I knew I wanted to move ahead and away from others deciding how good I was and what I was capable of achieving.

In fact, what I wanted was "the good life"—the life that everyone else seemed to be experiencing. I wasn't necessarily focused on lots of money. I guess I just wanted to prove myself to myself and, of course, to everyone else. My mother would always say, "You're never satisfied." She was right.

Anita had already learned how bad life could be with its unexpected shocks and cold, cruel surprises. You would think it would have made her very cautious and wary of people and things, but she was an example of survival of the fittest: she adapted. She maximized her strengths and learned to live with the fact that her eye would be an object of interest to young and old. In high school her face was still changing and becoming her woman's face. She knew about makeup and how to do her hair. She created great styles with her longish blonde hair and elastic bands. She was a cheerleader and she played basketball like she knew what she was doing. But no matter how accomplished, no matter how prepared she was, embarrassing, disappointing things still happened to her and I, yet again, was absolutely no help.

In addition to hiking our uniforms up at St. Pat's we also wore nylons under our skirts to give our knee-high socks a more sophisticated look. These were real nylons, the kind that require a garter belt. The garter belt was a complicated piece of underwear. You wore it around your waist, closing it at the back with hooks and eyes. It had four straps dangling down with rubber tabs and a hook that you used to keep the nylons up. The rubber hooks often broke off and then you used a penny with the hook. But this day Anita's garter belt had rubber tabs that were in place and the metal hooks hung down just the way they were supposed to. But, then, that's the thing about fate: it just waits for you to arrive and it happens.

Just as the bus pulled into the last stop on the bus loop and we stood up, Anita grabbed my hand and pulled me back down. "My garter belt is falling down," she hissed. Apparently the hook and eye at the back had finally given way.

"What do you want me to do?" What I meant was, "You're on your own."

She wanted me to ask someone for a safety pin. Oh, please. I couldn't go up to a stranger and ask for a pin. I didn't want to be connected with this stupid drama. I got off the bus and left her there.

She, of course, could not get off without her garter belt and nylons falling to her feet. There I stood behind the bus and watched her as she looked out the back window, the bus driving away with her still on it. I got on our connecting bus and went home without her.

I felt badly for her but *Hey, what could I do?* It was her garter belt. If it had been me she would have asked for a pin. But it wasn't me, and once again I felt that secret happiness that the bad thing was happening to someone else.

    She has said many times she forgives me for leaving her alone to solve that problem. She says it proves how self-sufficient she was. But I know how much it hurt her to be left like that and to be left by me. I was the one she thought she could trust. I was the one she thought would help her. Just shows you, doesn't it?

∼

Mum, Kathleen, Eileen, Tony, Mike, John - camping

Just Like Everyone Else

Sometimes it was too much to be one of so many. It gave me a stomach-ache, like too many green apples did. I wonder what kept Mom and Dad going? So much was unspoken about what they had to do that we drowned in the silent sound of what it meant to be such a large family. Nobody had to tell us that as tough as we had it Mom and Dad had it tougher. But we were children and all we wanted was to have fun, feel safe and be loved. For the most part, against all odds, we had that triangle of comfort.

They weren't big drinkers, big smokers or big gamblers. They focused their energy on the family unit. They were unreservedly old-fashioned, with everything that word conjures up. They believed that since they had brought us into the world they needed to do a good job. We needed to be fed, and they found ways, usually buying in bulk long before it became a cool thing to do. They bought mountains of day-old bread and huge bags of powdered skim milk. I didn't know that milk wasn't supposed to be blue until I left home. By then it was too late for me to ever consider milk a beverage.

Thank God we were a cute lot and at least we could make them proud standing scrubbed clean and neatly dressed—we looked like a larger version of the Von Trapp family without lederhosen and pinafores. But, damn, we were a lot of work, so I guess you couldn't blame them for taking their fun where they could, even if it meant embarrassment for us.

Filing into church on Sunday morning they revelled in the fact that we took up two long pews. Dad was always in front, Mom right behind holding the baby of the moment, and then the rest of us.

Big ones near small ones to keep an eye on them. Our arrival always caused indulgent, slightly disapproving smiles.

"Oh, look. It's the Gojevićs," as in, "Oh, look. It's that family that doesn't know when to stop. Don't they know about birth control?" They were Catholic, too, Catholics who should have been following that papal directive regarding birth control if they were the good Catholics they claimed to be. They mocked Mom and Dad for doing what they were supposed to be doing. I guess they didn't see the irony in that.

If Mom and Dad were aware that everyone else did not consider our large family such a glorious thing, they never mentioned it, although there were some muttered comments about how conveniently some people forgot what the church had told them to do. "Sunday Catholics" my mom called them.

Our weekly trips to church in our home parish were big events, but not as big as going to church when we went camping. No matter that there were so many of us, no matter that we had to put everything in pillowcases, we were going to church dressed as if we were going to church. Just because we were camping was absolutely no excuse not to attend church. Dresses, hats, gloves and shoes were squished into those expanded pillowcases. Clothes were pulled out all wrinkly on a Sunday morning and worn whether we begged them not to make us or not. Then we filed into some little church in some little town that usually seats twenty and took up most of the rows.

Transporting us in general and especially on our camping trips was always a logistical feat. In the early years we had an old Pontiac my English uncle had left behind as a farewell gift. It worked fine. We piled the stuffed pillowcases in first and sat on them. Everything else went into the trunk or was lashed to the roof. We didn't go far on those early trips, although they seemed so long we could have been going to France. The really fun part about this car and what made it special was that you could see the road as it went by through the hole in the floor. It was a great distraction. None of us thought it was strange or dangerous; it was just part of the way things were.

We moved on to an International Harvester van. It was dark-forest green and had the advantage of having plenty of room inside.

It would have been good for transporting lots of boxes of something. It didn't have any seats, or windows, either, except for the two small ones in the back door that didn't open. There was no air. Dad built benches inside, and there we sat bouncing along like so many smuggled refugees getting more and more carsick. We took turns being sick because when someone throws up, even if you hadn't thought of it before, now it seems like a really good idea.

Our cars charted the families' financial fortunes. When things started looking up, we got the ultimate family vehicle: the Ford wood-panelled station wagon. It was a salmon pink beauty with seats for everyone if we didn't all travel together. If we did we just layered one or two kids on top of the older kids. This car had lots of windows, the better to see all of us. Whenever we stopped at a light you could see people staring at us, counting us, calling out to my father, "Hey, are all those yours?" When we travelled on the ferry the guy in the wicket would say, "How many you got in there, buddy?" Dad would pretend he didn't know and start counting us as if more could have snuck in while he wasn't looking. We would scrunch down so we couldn't be seen, burning with teenage embarrassment. In truth we were so thrilled to be out of the "Van from hell" that we never complained except to each other.

Along with the new wagon came the purchase of a used tent-trailer. Now this was a step up, an incredible piece of luxury. It partially replaced our well-lived-in tents. There was one huge cabin-shaped canvas that the kids slept in, lined up like sardines, head to toe. That bag had been stored all winter and when it was unfurled the smell was an overpowering mix of mouldy canvas, dirt and just the faintest whiff of something that reminded me of dried pee with an undertone of old boys' socks. Often after rainy nights you would wake up with the walls dripping and a big puddle in the middle of the tent that had got there by running underneath our sleeping bags and us. Then the recriminations would fly.

"Okay, who touched the tent?" "I'm telling; you know you aren't supposed to touch the tent when it's raining." Of course we all had touched the tent. How could you not touch the tent when Dad had warned us, "If you touch you the tent when it's raining it will weep.

Just leave it alone and the rain won't come through. You kids are always touching it and then you come crying to us. Don't touch it!"

Mom, Dad and the baby of the moment in its playpen slept in relative peace and comfort in their own tent right beside us. Nobody was touching the tent in there.

Often we arrived at a campsite after it was dark and had to set up those tricky, unwieldy tents in the pitch black. There were so many poles and so many ways to connect them that weren't right. Then there were the anchor pins, which only worked if you got them into just the right kind of soil. Too hard and there would be fruitless hammering, too soft and they pulled out in the middle of the night leaving one side sagging, threatening to suffocate one or more of us.

It was hard to get your bearings in an unlit campsite, and often the tent was set up on a slant or in a bit of a dip or on top of tree roots. These Braille tent erections were works of hope and faith. It was inevitable that some poor schmuck would get the tree root under his or her sleeping bag, in the middle of the night crawl in with someone else, and be treated to intense grousing in the morning.

One particularly grim night we arrived in the dark and it was raining. This was the perfect combination required to make putting up a tent a nightmare. Things proceeded with lots of banging and clanging and shouting and crying and general mayhem. Eventually we all ended up inside the tent. Very soon, however, it became clear that something was very, very wrong. We were used to dampness and wet but this was different. This was "a river runs through it." I wasn't happy about it and no one else was, either. But we were sleepy and weren't about to jump up and do anything about it.

Helena did. She went outside and she and Dad by the glow of the Coleman lantern dug a trench around the tents so the rain had somewhere to go besides under us.

So, yes, that tent-trailer was a beautiful thing. We couldn't all sleep in it but it did mean a dry place to cook and somewhere to hide out if it was raining. Most of all it was one more step on the road to the fabled land of the middle class—a place we all longed to be a part of.

~

Mom – pregnant

Driving Crazy

Mom liked that tent-trailer of ours the best because she could do her shameful breast-feeding out of the public eye. She didn't need to go through intricate cover-ups so the sight of a baby breast-feeding wouldn't offend people. Dad was ambivalent. He liked the fact that there wasn't quite so much drama around tents now, but it did call upon driving skills he had never fully mastered.

It was a searing hot day. We had been heading down a highway Dad was sure was a shortcut to where we wanted to go. It did appear as a red squiggly line on the map, an indication of an unpaved road, but Dad had great faith in the Canadian highway system.

"In Canada if it isn't a four-lane highway they think it's impassable. It's probably just a little potholed."

Great clouds of dust swirled around us. I glanced around; we were covered in so much dust we looked like we were auditioning to compete in a Marcel Marceau look-alike contest. Brendan had already thrown up twice. Mom was seething and stone-faced in the front seat. It would be pointless to state the obvious to Dad: that this had been a bad move. He finally came to that conclusion by himself. This was not just a dusty, unpaved road; it was more of a donkey track with nowhere to turn around safely, even if you knew how to turn around safely with a tent-trailer in tow.

Dad told us all to get out of the car. We weren't sure why. There we stood at the side of the road looking like a pack of scruffy, dirty dogs while he unhitched the trailer so he could turn the station wagon around. The trailer was loaded down with the things that used to go on top of the car: the hundred-pound wooden chest he had built for the food was full of tins of jam and peanut butter and spaghetti sauce and ten-pound bags of sugar. There were camp stoves and lanterns in there, every cast iron pot and pan we owned, hammers, saws, screwdrivers and mauls. There were clothes and shoes for fourteen people and of course the tents, their pegs and pins and miles of rope. The wheels of that laden trailer sank into the sun-softened tar.

Once Dad had completed the car U-turn he explained our roles. Mom, the baby and the little kids were to stand by as eager, frightened spectators. The rest of us had to pick up the fully loaded tent-trailer, drag it behind us and run like hell with it across the highway in case a car was to come upon us without warning. So that's what we did, looking like a very strange collection of Third World taxi drivers. The fact that he couldn't negotiate turning the car and the trailer around together was no big deal; it was just that we were ill prepared for that unexpected dose of reality.

"Oh," it slowly dawned on us, "Dad doesn't always know what he's doing." It was a shocking, unnerving revelation. We thought, like most kids, that Dad knew everything about everything. Turns out he didn't. We were under no such illusions when it came to Mom and the road.

Mom learned to drive in her fashion and probably shouldn't have. She had gotten along just fine for many years but she couldn't leave well enough alone. When you say that someone drives it implies a certain competence, but she never had it. Rules were for the others, as were speed limits and all other accepted ways of being on the road. Signalling was unnecessary.

"I am moving my car over. Can't he see that I want to get into that lane?"

She sat up very straight and very close to the wheel, which she held in a death grip so it couldn't get away. She stared straight ahead with manic concentration. She didn't appear to take in much more than four square inches of the windshield in front of her. The car was, mercifully, an automatic. The skill involved in coordinating clutches and brakes, lights and turn signals, shoulder checks and lane changes would have been impossible.

And then she put her foot to the pedal. We lurched forward and slowed down, lurched forward and slowed down, and that was the way it was for the remainder of any trip with her. We'd go around a corner very, very slowly aaaaand lurch, slow down. You couldn't speak to her while she was driving. She didn't even yell at us; that would have been far too distracting.

Now if *you* were driving that was another matter. Her hand gripping the door handle, right foot firmly pressing her phantom brake pedal, she gave out a non-stop stream of directions and dire warnings.

"Look out, there's a car up there." "Can't you see that red light?" "Why are you driving so fast?" "Slow down." Then she would reach over, grab your arm, digging in her nails, and pull you so the car swerved. She would yell, "You're going to kill us all driving like that!"

She didn't like hills, backing up, parallel parking or driving on the freeway—you had to go way too fast. She would drive around and around and around the block to find a spot she could just drive right into. She had lots of accidents. They were other peoples' fault.

"Honestly," she would say, "they didn't give any indication at all that they were going to stop until they did. I mean, really, you should give a person more warning." And she meant it in the self-righteous way only really bad drivers can manage. You could tell she hated driving, and she didn't do it for very long. But, my God, while she was driving the world was not a safe place.

What began as a rebellious move on her part turned out to be her nemesis. Driving was her stab at feminism. She no doubt would have given it up sooner if it hadn't been for Timothy.

∼

Timothy Patrick Gojević

Surprise

Timothy was the youngest, number twelve, and the sixth boy, at last evening things up. With his birth there were finally six girls and six boys. There has always been the suggestion, started by Mom, that if I had been a boy, as she was sure I was going to be, they wouldn't have ended up with a family of twelve children.

I was born at home in a living room in Huyton on Roby, just outside Liverpool, England. In 1951 lots of kids were born at home. Dad had created a birthing room downstairs. He had brought the bed from upstairs, and on that very cold night had built a huge fire in the living room fireplace. The midwife was there and there were lots of sheets warming. Mom was propped up in bed.

"Go to bed now," she told the three older ones, "and when you get up in the morning Paul will be here."

So it's going to be a boy, they all thought. Good—that would even things out: two girls and two boys. And Peter would have a playmate and maybe he would stop getting into trouble. (It wasn't until they had six children, however, that they had another boy, and by then Peter had a well-established routine of criminal behaviour that no number of little brothers was going to fix.)

When they got up in the morning everyone wanted to see him, this new little boy.

"Where is he? Where's Paul?"

"Not Paul, Pauline," my mother said.

No one has ever said what tone she used when she delivered this news. But she did say many times over the years, "You know, if you had been a boy that would have been perfect. Two girls, two boys."

She said that was what she had been striving toward. I guess everybody has to have a goal. Then she delivered the kicker.

"Then we wouldn't have had any more children."

What, you mean eight more children were brought into this world simply because I was a girl? Now, that is power. A kind of twisted power but, you know, I'll take it.

Mom and Dad were together for about two weeks after they married and then he sailed away for a few months. When he returned he was shocked to find out she wasn't already pregnant.

"Is something wrong with you?" he asked. It certainly couldn't be him.

Fortunately when he returned next time, she was pregnant, which began a long, long love affair with her hormones. Every nineteen months or so they surged and there she was "in a family way" again.

Mom got pregnant with Timothy when she was forty-two and well past her best-before date for reproduction. Brendan, who was number eleven, thought, and so did everyone else, that he would always be the baby. He was so beautiful with his white blonde hair and pointy little elf chin it seemed that would have been a good place to call it quits. He was five years old and Mom had been pregnant off and on for ninety-nine months. She had been having babies since she was nineteen, and that five-year gap between Brendan and Timothy was the longest time she had ever not been pregnant.

She was really good at getting pregnant, and I don't think she thought it was strange that she was pregnant the same time as Helena, her oldest child. They waddled around together with big bellies and swollen ankles. Mom offered Helena all kinds of unsolicited advice. She made it pretty clear to Helena that she had the market cornered on pregnancy and all its details. It was hard to argue the fact. After all, she had had eleven live, vaginal births, with no twins. She knew what to expect and when to expect it. She knew the signs and portents, the markers and stages.

Objects in Mirror Are Closer than They Appear

At least she said she did. She was shocked when Timothy was born and he "wasn't quite right." Later she admitted he had never moved around much when she was pregnant. He lay in her belly a very still, very quiet little peanut just waiting to be born and yell, "Surprise!"

When she asked to see him the doctor told her maybe that wasn't a good idea.

"Why, does he have two heads?" she asked.

"He has Down's syndrome," the doctor replied. He could have said he has horns and blue skin. Neither she nor Dad knew what Down's meant or what they were supposed to do about it. All that it meant to have Down's became clear as the years went on, but for now they lingered in their innocent ignorance.

"It would be better for everyone if you just let us put him in a home. He will never improve and he will probably not see his twelfth birthday anyway."

That, of course, is what they did back then: hid away the not-perfect kids. To have a child like that was shaming, and you certainly wouldn't want everyone to see him and judge him or you.

Where had that doctor been when Mom first got pregnant with Timothy? He certainly hadn't shared with her that older women getting pregnant stand a very good chance of giving birth to a child with Down's. He probably knew it wouldn't have mattered even if he had told her. She never would have done anything about it.

She just replied in a very matter-of-fact voice, "Don't be ridiculous. He is our child and he is coming home with us."

She and Dad showed the bravest of faces, but when the doctor left they cried. They cried for the baby that wasn't like the others. This was a baby that would have a life not quite up to scratch. But they also cried for themselves.

"What the hell next?" they thought. "After all we have been through, and now a kind of broken baby."

They didn't stay in that place of mourning long, though. There was a nurse who came around, saw them weeping for their child and gave them a little poem. It was doggerel, really, with lots of rhyming lines. There was something hopeful in those lines, reminding them they were above all else really good at raising kids and they would do the same for Tim.

Anyway, Mom loved babies. When they were tiny and helpless she was most engaged. She often said that the long hours spent breast-feeding were her happiest moments. Sweet little ones smelling of baby powder and that wonderful baby scent, babies who needed her—this was where she shined. A baby was special, something to be treasured and, let's face it, they pretty much did as they were told.

Mom was raised by a mother who certainly did not believe in excesses of emotion. Even her father's doting couldn't counteract the belief her mother instilled in her that showing emotion was a failure of character. Ah, but babies. Here was a legitimate time and place to squander your love and affection. It must have been a blessed relief to hold those infants of hers and lose herself in the passionate joy of loving without reserve.

From the time you could crawl, however, you started to lose that primary place and begin to be absorbed into the large corpus of the Family Gojević. The ones just above you became your playmates and primary caregivers. By the time most of us reached nineteen months Mom was pregnant again anyway, so there was just no lingering in babyhood.

So Tim the newest baby, the afterthought baby, came home. He was a tiny, funny-looking, barely moving bundle. He had little almond-shaped eyes. He was all soft and floppy like a Cabbage Patch doll with the telltale sign of a single crease on his palms. He was not just another baby. He had to sleep sitting up with a vaporizer going because he was always wheezing, his little nose stuffed up and his eyes red-rimmed like a small mouse's. The house always smelled like a Vicks cough drop. He took hours to feed, and it became clear very quickly that this was going to be the "shared baby." Everybody had to be actively involved in his life.

We decided the best thing to do was just to spoil the hell out of him. As Dad said, "He has enough to deal with. We will just love him."

Here was a little boy that Dad, especially, could pour endless amounts of affection and attention onto and feel no guilt over spoiling or indulging. He was never left to cry, unlike the other babies who had been allowed to really exercise their lungs. He was always held and rocked and sung to. He was so sweet and easy to love. He would lie in the crook of your arm and just stare off into the middle distance. There was none of that pesky flailing of arms and legs that most babies engage in.

As it took more time to reach every other milestone, it took him a long time to learn to crawl. At first he rocked in place, back and forth, rubbing his knees raw. It took him a long time to figure out the forward-motion principle. But when he did, he celebrated with perpetual motion. He was everywhere at once, but mostly in cupboards pulling out and banging pots and pans.

"Oh, isn't that cute?" we all said, and meant it. He went into food cupboards and made big, gooey piles of brown sugar and syrup. He played in flour and water and made paste that he smeared on walls and cupboards. He was a very small, very powerful bulldozer moving through the house, leaving a trail of destruction and mess behind him. We were thrilled that he was "exploring his world," acting like a regular baby. Except regular crawling babies would have had limits. Tim was a limitless baby.

The neighbours had a slightly different take on his behaviour, especially when he went into their cupboards and commenced to turn their floor into a peanut butter and jam sandwich. Once Tim discovered mobility he became the Harry Houdini of the diaper set. You could not keep him in his crib or his room or the house. He was pliable, like Gumby, and could ooze himself out of his crib, between small cracks in doors, under security gates. He could have joined the circus.

Tim began his first solo adventures crawling out the back door and sliding on his tummy, face first, down the stairs. He had a permanent scrape on his forehead and nose from landing on his face. Then there was more crawling over the grass to the neighbour's house and directly into their kitchen, where he proceeded to empty out everything he could lift. The inevitable phone call—"He's over here again"—sent someone running to get him.

These neighbour calls joined a whole collection of other phones calls we would get about him. "Tim is heading down the street," "Tim is riding his trike toward the entrance to the freeway," and the most frequent from the local hospital emergency department: "He's up here again. You will find him on bed five."

Unlike many people, Tim loved the hospital. By now he was walking on his very short, sturdy little legs that took him up to the hospital near our house. He loved going in there and getting "checked out." The nurses listened to his heart and let him get on the bed to be covered up, where he would be happy to lie for a very long time.

He was a lucky little boy. He did things that would have had real consequences for other kids, but he bounced along unaware. There was one time, though, when he wasn't so lucky. Somehow he had managed yet again to get out of the house unseen. This time he ended up on the driveway and was run over by one of the guys working for Dad at the time, who said he had been alerted by the "thump, thump" and then Tim's weak cry. He slammed on the brakes, jumped out, and there was Tim mewing like a kitten.

Mom ran out, scooped him up and rushed to the hospital with him. She probably shouldn't have picked him up, but that's what a mother does. It was a miracle he didn't die. Instead, the top of his foot was crushed. And in the parlance of war, there was some collateral damage to others.

Mike, an older brother by a few years, was supposed to be looking after Tim. The tricky guy that Tim was evaded detection as he slipped by, and that is why he ended up in the driveway. Decades later Mike remembers that day with a painful clarity. Mom was uncharacteristically hysterical and he was horrified at the events. He saw Mom as not just angry but truly, maybe for the first time, totally bereft. And what is a young boy to do about events so hugely out of his control?

He said to Kathleen, "Here, take this dime. Go and buy Mom a chocolate bar." He understood the terrible nature of what had happened. In his mind a chocolate bar would make things all right again, make his mom happy again and maybe bring back safety and the familiar.

When they brought Tim home he wasn't crying anymore, but he had weird bruises in exactly the same pattern as the tire treads on his arms and legs and a large bandage on his foot. His floppy little body had saved him by moulding like putty under the tire. It wasn't the first or last time that not being perfect turned out to be just the thing.

I don't know if Mom and Dad agonized over Tim. I thought it was odd there were no hints of Catholic guilt, the old "He must have been sent as a punishment for something." At least we never heard it from Mom and Dad. Coming out of church one day I did overhear someone say, "Gee, you think they would have quit while they were ahead. Now look what they got."

Mom and Dad, at least in public, adhered to the a-disabled-child-is-a-gift-from-God school of thought. It is bad form, after all, to complain about a gift. I never heard any wailing or gnashing of teeth or any cries of "Why us?"

In other folks this might have been seen as very stoic—brave and noble, even—and it was. But perhaps Mom and Dad thought that since they already had eleven semi-normal kids it was just their turn. I'm also inclined to believe there was something in both of them that saw the joy in Tim, and they embraced him as their last best chance.

∼

B. Eileen, John, Helena, Tony, Mary Anne, Mike and Brendan
F. Pauline, Peter, Anita, Timothy, Kathleen

Gone Cruisin'

Mom and Dad had been married for thirty-five years and had twelve children when Dad experienced a raging mid-life crisis. Someone no one knew, especially himself, replaced the hyper-responsible man he was. He had been diagnosed with diabetes in his 40s and, boy, did that shake him to his core. Diabetes had him in a good firm grip and it required a full life-changing routine. He loved sweets and that was out. More than that was the requirement for carefully balanced meals containing all the right nutrients.

We've already talked about Mom's cooking and the strain that creating those meals caused her. She did figure out three meals for Dad that fulfilled the requirements. Breakfast: cereal, toast and coffee. Lunch: ham and cheese on whole-wheat bread. Dinner: a huge steak, a baked potato and green peas. Every day. Sounds like culinary prison.

Anyway, he never complained about what was served. Maybe he should have. Maybe he should have bought himself a little red sports car or taken up scuba diving. Mom should have been suspicious that he didn't complain, since that was his usual behaviour. He complained about a lot of things, especially the rise of feminism and how it was ruining the family unit.

"The family can't have two bosses. I am the boss and your mother is my first in command."

It wasn't as simple as "a woman's place is in the kitchen," though. For Dad it was more a meddling with the natural order of the universe. Some things were just meant to be. His belief in what was man's work and what was woman's work around the house was pretty clear too. Girls polished the boys' shoes (including Peter's), helped with cooking, cleaned the house, babysat and did anything else that needed doing. Boys took out the garbage and cut the grass. This was Dad's version of a fair division of labour.

But Dad couldn't change the course of feminism and couldn't convince Mom of her wrong-headedness. He also couldn't get her to do all the things she had done in the past without question. He had liked the way she ironed his shirts, the way his food came to the table first, the way his ideas were highlighted and extolled. He liked all these little attentions, and things were changing in ways he knew he could not stop.

So he got himself a mistress. Not just any mistress. This woman belonged to our church. Why do they always belong to the church? She was a very non-feminist-leaning woman. She and her husband also volunteered at the church bingo along with Mom and Dad.

She didn't look like anyone's mistress. True, she was British like Mom and buxom like Mom. In every other way she was definitely not like Mom. She was younger by about twenty-five years. Her two front teeth leaned on each other like two guys taking a rest. She dressed in tweedy skirts and sensible shoes that made her look older than she was. Maybe that was the whole idea—to look more like an age-appropriate mate for Dad. She had an old-lady hairdo but I don't think Dad was looking at her do. She was a home economist, no surprise there. And, oh—she doted on Dad.

She baked him diabetic cookies and cakes; she was always giving Mom sugar-free recipes. That didn't tip off Mom either, though, because people were always giving her recipes (which she promptly lost or threw away). Mom liked this woman. In fact she probably counted her a friend. She came on the family boat for weekend outings and brought along the food.

By the time the affair reached its peak we kids had left home except for Tim and the second-youngest, Brendan. We were for the most part totally unaware that things were hurtling downhill between Mom and Dad. That is one of the side effects of living a tumultuous life; you can't always tell from the outside when things are going sideways. Not that they were always yelling and shouting and throwing things. In fact, their marriage seemed to have settled into comfortable routines.

This is the way the story should have gone: Immigrants, after having sold all their possessions, arrive in Canada with $35 in their pockets. They proceed to work like slaves at whatever jobs they can find. They have twelve children. They are pillars of their church. They tithe. They become financially stable. Life is good. They grow old together. And the sun sets in the west as a rich, romantic Bach adagio plays in the background.

Except that this script was directed by some angst-ridden Bulgarian who saw bleakness and despair everywhere and decided at the last moment things were going along all too well. "Where's the pathos?" he demanded. So he had Dad run off with a woman half Mom's age.

Running off sounds energetic and exciting. Actually, he told Mom he "needed some time by himself." He slipped quietly away to a big city across the country. Mom still didn't clue in. He was going to work there, he said, and gather his thoughts and do the usual "re's." Reassess, re-evaluate, renew. At the time we all thought, *How very modern of him*. He was taking time away to get centred and would come back refreshed and ready to resume his married life.

Secretly, though we never said it to Mom, we also thought, *Yeah, the poor guy. He needs a break, a little distraction after a lifetime of hard work and sacrifice.* We were always a bit more forgiving of him than Mom. He always seemed a more tragic figure somehow. He was the noble hunter-gatherer while she was cast firmly in the role of whining harridan.

She, too, thought he was just having a little break. She may even have thought he was having a fling. He'd had them before, apparently. Mom said she hadn't minded those. He always came back to her and, well, "A man has needs." What she didn't know was that he had arranged to meet his lover in the city. After a few months he called Mom to tell her he wasn't coming back.

When she told me what Dad had decided she said it in the very flat voice sometimes used by those in shock.

"You know I had a dream about your father and that woman."

"You did?" I said, believing I should encourage her to "open up."

"Yes," she continued. "It seemed so real but when I woke up I thought, *Oh, just a dream*. But it wasn't a dream, so I guess this means I'm clairvoyant."

I didn't say, "Well, I think you've probably known all along that something was going on but it was a bit tough to admit that your husband was having an affair right under your nose. So you wilfully chose to ignore it, hoping it, like all the others, would just go away."

Mom wasted no time in dealing with her shock and sorrow. She created her own action plan, which she strictly adhered to for the next two-and-a-half years: berate Dad, berate the other woman, retell the same anguishing tale of betrayal over and over again, drink lots of red wine. Repeat as needed.

During this time she moved out of our family home and went to live in a tall high-rise building a few floors down from my brother Tony and his wife, Arlene.

Brendan, meanwhile, had made the mistake of going out of town to work after high school. When he came home there wasn't one. It shook him to the core. Not only wasn't there a home, all the things that were in the house were either in a dumpster or with Mom. Dad took nothing.

We were all too busy to notice Brendan's pain. Since then he has talked about the horror of that time. He says he thinks we were cruel to act so uninterested in his fate. It wasn't really so much cruelty, however, as the fact that there seemed to be bigger fish to fry. We were, for instance, taken up with the notion of what it meant not to have a mom and dad together. Us, the Gojevićs, a "broken family." Impossible. We were a cliché in the way we reacted, each of us totally absorbed in how it was affecting us and totally oblivious to the reaction of the others. We weren't mean, just self-absorbed.

It began for a Brendan a short interval of living here, there and everywhere. There was a combination of couch surfing, living with one or other brother or sister and, finally, at nineteen he got married. Now he had a home again.

Some would say Tim wasn't as lucky as Brendan. He stayed and got to live with Mom. This apartment was as different from her past life as she could make it. It was small and the door was always locked. Visits there were always unsettling. In this too-hot, stuffy, two-bedroom apartment she had crammed most of the furniture that had fit into the house. There was the same stuff—the orange and brown floral sofa, the lamps with the curly shades, the "Colonial" end tables and coffee table, the tall hutch filled with knick-knacks—but somehow everything seemed smaller and unfamiliar. The walls were covered in family pictures of all of us except, of course, Dad.

Mom reverted to her favourite defrost-before-eating, just-add-water cooking. Fortunately for her, Tim was not a discerning eater. If it was chicken it was good. If it was Shake and Bake chicken it was really good. Tim ballooned with chicken, instant mashed potatoes and frozen corn.

His bedroom was his other safe zone. He went in there and put on his headphones and listened to Elton John's "Rocket Man" and Neil Diamond's "Soolaimon" for as long as Mom would let him. His eczema went haywire. He scratched and scratched and the white flakes fell in a snowstorm of sadness.

The truth was that Mom wanted to do just what Tim was doing, which wasn't much. Her preferred activity at this time was to sit in her favourite stuffed lounger and fill in the crossword puzzle in the paper. She had the luxury of behaving this way, as she didn't need to work. Dad sent along guilt money in the beginning. Then they sold the family house and she was given the lion's share. No doubt she and Dad both thought it was her due. During the early days she talked of taking on a part-time job. "Just one or two days a week," she said. It never happened.

What she did do was stay up to watch cheesy movies and sleep in late. In some ways she and Tim were perfectly suited; he liked sleeping as much as she did. In all her life Mom said she had never had enough sleep. All those babies, all those late-night feeds, and kids with middle-of-the-night stomach aches. Now she could sleep as long as she liked. It was also something to do while she figured out what the hell she was going to do with the rest of her life without Dad.

It wasn't surprising, therefore, that Mom was home in her apartment the day my brother Tony died and rose from the dead. He apparently had been sitting at his dining room table, made a gurgling noise and then melted onto the table. Arlene called 911 and then Mom. Mom took one look at Tony and began her version of CPR. She later said she saw someone doing something just like it on a TV emergency-room drama. Who says TV is a waste of time? It must have worked because when the ambulance arrived and they pulled out those paddles to shock him back to life he wasn't brain-dead yet. They said it was a good thing Mom had kept that trickle of oxygen to his system.

They took him off to the hospital, where they discovered that at twenty-five he had had a heart attack caused by an electrical disturbance, like a toaster with fried wires. We waited two days for him to wake up, wondering if he would speak in sentences and know who we were. He did, and when I asked him if he had seen a bright light and if he had wanted to go toward it he said, "No white light, no nothing."

I was very disappointed. This would have been a great opportunity to find out first-hand what, if anything, was going on in the universe. Tony felt a bit cheated, too, because he had heard that sometimes people who are in that special state between life and death leave their bodies and float above, looking down on themselves thinking, *Am I dead?* Nothing like that happened to Tony either. Except for Mom's heroic rescue, it was a fairly boring Lazarus story.

When Mom wasn't saving her son she was drinking. She was partial to the large jug wines. She reasoned that after the first five or six glasses the bouquet didn't really matter. She liked being drunk; getting there gave her something to do and was a fine alternative to what her real life was offering.

We all thought this plan of action was a pretty good one and certainly understandable under the circumstances. Here was a woman who had been with the same man since she was eighteen, had twelve children with him, helped him start up and develop a successful business, saw him and all of us through crisis upon crisis and then is left for a younger woman. This new lifestyle of hers seemed to be suiting her well until she wandered drunk out onto the street one day. The next-door neighbour had seen her swaying toward the road and yelled to her. She apparently glanced up, quite startled to find herself there. Up until that point we had been walking around with our fingers in our ears, saying, "La, la, la," and then we started to pay attention.

The problem was that Mom had an almost pathological need to keep telling the tale of her horror, worrying away at it like a canker in her mouth. It really hurt but she just couldn't stop herself. And honestly, after the thirtyth time, we were fairly tired of it. In her telling there was the unspoken need to have us say that yes, Dad was the complete and utter asshole and it was entirely his fault.

But just like the divisions over Peter, there were different schools of thought about Dad's culpability. For some there were extenuating circumstances. The key idea expressed by this group was, "He must have been so unhappy and we wouldn't want him to stay in an unhappy marriage." Another group just blamed Mom. "Well, if she hadn't always been on his case maybe he would have stayed around. He just wanted some peace."

In a strange twist, Peter declared he thought Dad was a hypocrite. "Here he is giving me shit about my lifestyle and he's been having affairs for years. And now he runs off with another woman." Oh, the self-righteous anger was a thing to behold. When all you've ever done your whole life is the wrong thing there is nothing quite as satisfying as pointing the finger of guilt at someone else.

Mom didn't have many totally committed supporters cheering for her in her corner. But everyone felt sorry for her, even the folks who thought she brought it on herself—especially the women who knew that being left for another woman was always a possibility. It was just such a cliché to be left by your husband for a younger woman that listening to her was like watching a bad daytime soap. Just like those soaps, there was no end in sight.

Someone finally said to her, "Kathleen, maybe you should go and talk to someone about all this."

"Talk? Talk? What am I going to say? My husband got tired of my old, flabby body and chose someone with a younger one? Or, my husband decided I wasn't fun enough or interesting enough or a good enough cook, so he went and found someone who was? I am embarrassed enough—do I need to tell the whole world my sorry tale?"

"But telling a third party would be so helpful, Kathleen. They don't know you or Pero. Maybe a fresh pair of eyes, a new perspective?"

People say stupid things when they don't know what to say. It's bad enough when someone has died and we try to find words of comfort. What do you say to her when someone she loved may as well have been dead but wasn't. Instead this person she has loved and lived with her whole adult life is off having a wonderful time somewhere else while she, the one left behind, suffers and suffers and says things like, "He threw me away like an old, used shoe."

Mom did finally go to see someone, once. It only took once because Mom, the ever-practical one, heard what she needed to hear.

Therapist: "So, what are you going to do with the rest of your life?"

Mom: "I don't know. All I have ever known how to do was be his wife and a mother to my children."

Therapist: "Well, is there anything you've always wanted to do? You could do it now; you can choose."

Mom: "I've always wanted to go on a cruise.

Therapist: "So go on a cruise."

It was as simple as that: cruising as therapy. Mom came home and said she had enjoyed her time with the therapist. Oh, and she was going on a cruise to Hawaii.

Mom had never been anywhere in her life alone. In fact, she hadn't been alone since she had married at eighteen. No one really thought she would do it. But she did, and she prepared for it like she was going into battle. Hair salon—check. Pedicure/manicure—check. Matching cruise wear—check. Fancy dresses—check. And off she went.

We heard later that there were many little glitches between leaving home and finally making it onto the ship. She handled everything. Of course she did; she had handled a family of twelve. Lost luggage and misdirection were peanuts. It's still odd to think of her alone negotiating Customs, and finding where to go and what to do. It wasn't that she wasn't clever; we knew she was. It was just a failure of imagination on our parts to see her in a different setting. We couldn't imagine a place where she was responsible to no one but herself. She loved it. She was at heart a problem solver, a charmer.

All her youthful behaviour came back. She found her rounded British tones worked magic on the Americans on the ship. She looked every bit a tastefully dressed, elegant traveller. Picture her, a lovely, older woman on the upper deck of the ship leaning over the railing smiling and waving—free, with no one to tell her what to do or when to do it. Finally, there was no one to ask her to do something for them. No meals to cook, no children to corral. At last just her and what she wanted. She said it was better than booze.

Bob noticed her right away. He was, as they say, enchanted. They were inseparable for the entire cruise. She showed him pictures of her family; he showed her his. He was a widow and grieving just like Mom. She told him the Coles Notes version of the Dad situation.

He had been a happily married man living in southern California creating full and partial dentures. Now he was a widow. He told Mom he would be pleased to work on hers. (Now, that is romance.) They danced and sang and drank champagne. They walked around the deck of the ship and laughed. It would have been something to see. This was our mom, but better. When the cruise ended he returned to his sunny home and Mom returned to hers, a changed woman. He called her every day, sometimes twice a day. She called him and there was lots of giggling and laughing. He decided he needed to come up here and meet her family.

He was a small, dapper man, dressed in south coast casual, his very curly grey hair neatly combed back. For a denturist he had a surprising overbite. He was probably just proud because they were his own teeth and he was thrilled to show off their imperfections. We liked him, mainly because he seemed to like Mom. We were all for anything and anyone who made her happy, because we certainly weren't doing a very good job in that area.

Then, just like in a Harlequin romance novel, he asked her to marry him after a courtship of a few months. She, without hesitating, said yes. All her life she had made careful, prudent plans that considered the greater good, but now she could make plans that were all about her.

It did seem all a bit rushed, but it turned out there was some urgency. It seemed Bob had cancer. It had been in remission but had returned. It affected his eating but not his attitude. He was determined to be as happy as he could for as long as he could, and that plan included Mom.

They got married in a chapel in Lake Tahoe with a rented minister, lots of bouquets of fake flowers, and taped music. There's Mom with her fancy dress demurely lifted above her knee while Bob slips off the garter. They look the way two people look when they have no one else to answer to and are totally focused on happiness here and now. Mom loved her California lifestyle. They had parties and barbecues. They went on long drives along the coast and stopped at little restaurants for lunch. Mom missed us, I think, but she was so happy living *la vida loca*.

I know she missed Tim. Soon after the wedding Mom and Dad had decided that maybe now was the time for him to take a turn living with Dad and the new wife in small-town British Columbia. It all seemed so logical and sensible; a divorced couple can share in the living arrangements of the child. She wasn't thrilled that Tim was living with Dad, but what could she do? She had agreed to it, and California with its new kind of life was calling.

It turned out Tim loved living with Dad and the "other woman" (O.W.). Dad didn't nag him the way Mom used to. In Tim Mom had found the perfect outlet for her angst. She could rag on him all day and he would rarely complain. She found no end of things to go on about. They usually started the same way and ended with different options. "Timothy, you need to: (fill in the blank) dress faster, eat less, come out of your room, stop listening to that Neil Diamond record, stop watching that Star Wars movie for the millionth time. Hurry up.

It was the last one that really made her crazy. He cannot be hurried. He has only one speed, and that is very, very slow. Each movement requires careful consideration. Putting on his socks and shoes can take up to half an hour. First you roll the sock down like a large condom and then you put it on your foot and slowly roll it up.

Pause, take a breath, pick up shoe, put on shoe, sigh, arrange shoe on very wide, very short foot, and connect Velcro. Repeat. All the shouting in the world cannot hurry him.

It was ironic, really, that Mom, who next to Tim was the slowest-moving person on earth, should be stuck trying to get someone else into another gear. All her cajoling and harassing of Tim had given Mom the extra zing she needed to keep going before she met Bob. Tim gave her purpose and reason. She could imagine herself a young mother again taking care of her children. That was something she knew and was good at.

But now Tim had a new, calm life with Dad and the O.W. They had enrolled him in a high school in their small town. He went bowling and swimming and competed at the local level in Special Olympics activities. There are many pictures of the three of them, and very odd pictures they are. They kind of look like a family in the way a Picasso is kind of a picture of reality—family slightly reformatted. You may have wondered, looking at those pictures, how those people were connected. Perhaps the grey-haired guy was the father of the dowdy-looking woman, and certainly he must be the grandfather to the special-needs kid. There were lots of interpretations.

They must have been the source of some conversation, those three. I wonder how much Dad and the O.W. told everyone. Or did they just let them believe that Tim was their child? This is possible but kind of icky.

Dad still couldn't stay away from bingo. Even when he relocated he found a way to get connected to that damn game. At least now he was being paid for all the time he put in. When he had volunteered in the church they thought they had the perfect sucker. He worked endless hours for free. It filled a need in Dad to be in charge, to organize schedules and shifts. He loved dreaming up new schemes for bringing in the crowds. The bingo was highly successful.

Of course Dad thought he was respected, admired, appreciated. He was wrong. If you needed any more proof that religion corrupts, you only needed to look at the nasty mix created by church and bingo. There is ego, power and jealousy everywhere, and that church-run gambling outfit was no different. The hundreds of hours Dad put into that game to bring in funds for the church were rewarded by a general rousting out with no thanks from a group who didn't like the upstart immigrant. Dad didn't speak about how he was treated, just as most people who have had something deeply shaming happen never mention it.

Dad talked about bingo players as if they were not in control of themselves. Why would anyone voluntarily sit in a room so full of smoke you could barely see your hand in front of your face and then dab a piece of paper over and over again with a coloured sponge? Dad and Mom never played a game themselves. For Mom, bingo had become a symbol of the world's evils. It was at bingo that Dad met that woman.

"You know, I always thought he enjoyed his time running that bingo more than made sense. Now I know it wasn't the bingo; it was the boobs."

I always thought Dad had made a chump move in leaving Mom. The last five years of his life away from Mom and the rest of us, living with the O.W., were a mixture of angst, guilt and embarrassment. I guess for him the trade-off was worth it.

The first few years after he left town with the O.W., some of us, including me, wouldn't go visit him. There were, as I mentioned, factions. Some did go because, they said, "He's our Dad. We miss him." It wasn't that I was particularly in the Mom camp. It was just too much for me to see him with that woman. It felt disloyal.

One summer after he had been living in Penticton for two years I went to spend a week with him. It was just as awkward as you would expect it to be. She tried too hard. I tried to act as if this was just fine, what with me being a woman of the world and all. Dad didn't know what to do. He put on his gruff persona of old and tried to engage me in arguments. Anger was always his strong suit. But it felt very unreal and stilted. I had half hoped he would be happy, that he would talk about his new life like Mom spoke of hers. I wanted him to tell me that all he had given up was worth it; here was a woman he truly loved. He loved her enough to tear apart the family. He loved her enough to give up the things he had worked his whole life for. He loved her enough to give up his true treasure, his family.

I never heard those words. I never even heard them intimated. What I did hear him say, almost casually as I left, was, "I love you. Call me. Come again." I heard later from others that he had said the same things to them.

It's so silly. He wanted it all. He was finally just fed up with the sacrifices in his life and now it was his turn. Some turn. The Faustian aspect of his act aside, he just wasn't happy in those years away from Mom. Maybe, like a spoiled child, he enjoyed being waited on hand and foot and having his every need met. But for a man with as much soul as he had, it seemed a poor trade.

In his dying, however, Dad yanked back the little control and power he had left. After he had a heart attack and went into a deep, dark coma, his lingering gave us all time to come and be with him. We gathered around his hospital bed like so many supplicants. We could hardly believe the very still bundle in that bed was Dad. Dad was big and vigorous and loud—not that helpless, unmoving shape. But, still, there was that face, the wide forehead with the familiar creases, the rounded eyelids, and the incredibly bushy eyebrows valiantly sticking out in every direction, and the big, proud nose.

"Dad," I whispered, as if I could wake him. It was really more of a question.

There wasn't much to be done, so we kept his mouth moistened with a swab, rearranged his pillows, washed his face and torso with warm cloths. It was so intimate and unsettling considering we had never been that close to the details of his body before. I had a small suspicion he wouldn't really have liked it. But to us those things seemed so purposeful. We talked to him as if he could hear. There is a whole body of literature that declares that even totally nonresponsive people can hear you speak, and since no one had come back to tell us otherwise we clung to that. We sat around and talked and played cards and ate Kentucky Fried Chicken and told stories to and about him.

He lay there not moving, just breathing slowly and deeply in and out, in and out. We sat and watched his chest rise and fall for four days. He had a pacemaker, and the doctor said as long as it was on he would go on. We knew he would not want to have that little box in his chest keeping him going like some Energizer Bunny.

I'm sure there have been many uncomfortable death-room scenes. I think Mom and the O.W. just outside Dad's room arguing over whether to disconnect his pacemaker ranks right up there in the pantheon of very uncomfortable discussions.

Mom: "I know he would not want to be kept alive this way. I lived with him for most of my life. Remember that?"

O.W.: "I am not prepared to just give up on him."

Mom: "Give up, what are you talking about? He's brain-dead."

O.W.: "We don't know that for sure until he wakes up."

Mom: "He isn't going to wake up." And on and on...

It was a true clash of the titans. In one corner we have Mom, the abandoned wife of thirty-five years and the mother of his twelve children. In the other corner we have the O.W., who has nursed him for five years and faced ridicule and shunning to be with him. They spoke so calmly; Mom especially, using that voice she reserved for times she was really scared. Like the time she heard Peter screaming and ran out to the backyard to find he had impaled his groin on a sharp stick. There was lots of blood and lots of screaming but Mom just said, "Well, that needs looking after," and she took care of it.

Wisdom and the power of our numbers prevailed. The O.W. came around and agreed to disconnect the pacemaker. Dad kept on keeping on in spite of it. He was like an old wind-up clock. He still had some spring left in him and he would keep tick, tick, ticking away until he was good and ready to wind down.

After spending four days by his bedside with no end in sight, I left. I was doing some magical thinking, hoping he was going to wake up and say, "What? What are you all doing here? I'm fine. I want to go home." This declaration would either be preceded or followed by some fabulous Croatian swearing.

You know how you start to think that if you lit a cigarette it would make the bus come more quickly? I thought maybe if I flew home he would make that turn for the better just because I wasn't looking. Yes, I know: crazy. As I was flying home that morning and the plane rose above the clouds, I had the feeling of rushing air and I knew he had died. It wasn't a big thing. There was no music, no aura, no bands of angels; it was more like something very soft brushing against your arms. It left me feeling reassured and peaceful.

Dad in his head had been a focused, unwavering worker and in his heart a romantic. I was sorry he had ended up in a very unromantic situation. He was a complicated man. I can never say I knew him, or understood him or what motivated him. I am still not clear all these years later how I feel about him leaving Mom. I wish I could take a stand and declare to myself he was totally wrong, but I have made too many mistakes myself to be willing or able to judge him. What I do believe is that he felt what he was doing was wrong and selfish. We didn't need to tell him that.

I also knew with absolute certainty that he loved me and I knew his love didn't depend on me being successful, loving or dutiful. I was his daughter and that was enough. He'd told me once I was the only one who could make him laugh. I always thought that was the best thing he ever said to me.

Because he had lived most of his life in Vancouver and he also had a big following in his new small town, the decision was made to have two funerals—not ideal but understandable, and maybe in this day and age of win or lose a pretty decent solution. Except that this wasn't going to be a cremation with a tidy little urn. Dad had requested a coffin burial complete with high mass. So back I flew to the small town where plans were fully underway for the funeral of the century. First there were prayers the night before the funeral and then the dreaded viewing.

It doesn't matter how much has been written about the terrifying effect of viewing a dead body, the barbaric practice persists. Looked at with the clear eyes of logic it makes no sense. Why would you drain the fluids from a body then dress it up in its best clothes, put makeup on it, style the hair to give it that "lifelike look," stick it in a box and make everyone look at what used to be a person? I desperately didn't want to view that coffin, but I knew refusing would cast me as unfeeling, unloving and, worst of all, uncooperative. Being uncooperative is one transgression the family really frowns on. Incidents of uncooperativeness will follow you your whole life.

So in spite of utter dread I walked up and looked into the face of the body I knew was not my father. My father was a smart, handsome man with chocolate-brown eyes and a beautiful, lopsided smile. This thing was frozen and rigid. Dad had dentures; they must have been removed and replaced with stuffing that made the area above his lip puffy. The overall effect of his body, however, was flat and two-dimensional. There was no depth or breadth to this man. It's been years ago now but I can still see that pretend-Dad so clearly. It's not a nightmare, just something pervasively awful and insidious. The sight of my father in that box floats back quite unbidden. I'm very sorry I looked.

The next day was the mass with the singing and sitting and standing and singing and sitting and standing. There were speeches, too, most of which I don't remember. I do remember leaving the church as sick and sad as I have ever been, then turning to my sister Eileen and saying, "Help me, hold me."

It was a terribly embarrassing thing to say to someone as private as Eileen. She had been one of the "I'm in Dad's camp" siblings from the earlier days. She had called him and visited him and defended him to the rest of us. I think she thought I was a bit of a Johnny-come-lately in the grieving department and really too much over the top. I don't mean to suggest that Eileen wasn't incredibly sad over losing Dad, but her way of showing it was more controlled. She grieved in her own way.

I think I may have reminded her a bit of those women in the black-and-white photos they sent to Dad from Dubrovnik when his mom died. There they are, dressed in black, draped over Grandmother Gojević's coffin and looking completely undone. That is how I felt— undone and emotional with so many tears and so much grief that

I really wanted to wail like those women were probably wailing in that picture.

But this was North America and people don't wail at funerals, especially at Catholic funerals. My falling apart in Eileen's arms was the height of my public display of emotion. After that I kept it to quietly crying, which was much more acceptable to the rest of the crowd. Many of the other family members were similarly overwrought and looked at me with sympathy. There are times when the only good response is one that might make others uncomfortable.

Following this feast of tears we all went on to the obligatory meet-and-greet with those who had come to eat the white triangle sandwiches with the crusts cut off and the too-sweet Nanaimo bars and to drink the bitter coffee and cold tea. I wanted a real drink badly. We got through it, it was awful, but what came next was worse.

I don't remember whom, and it doesn't really matter, but someone decided that the best thing to do now would be to close up the coffin and ship poor old Dad back to Vancouver from Penticton for another funeral. *"Pero Gojević and his Travelling Body Road Show."*

Part Two, Vancouver Funeral: prayers, viewing, funeral and gathering. Only this time I refused to go to the viewing. Screw them all; there was no way I was going to go and look at Dad again. He would no doubt be worse for the wear from travelling in that new, wooden hinged home of his. Flip open the lid and there he is again in all his made-up glory. I talked to my brother Tony, who did look before Dad was put on display for the second time. During the lifting and moving some shifts had naturally taken place. Tony noticed that one of Dad's hands had moved away from being crossed on his chest and now was clinging to his crotch. He said it gave him the creeps, but it also gave Dad a lively look, as though he were just about to do something interesting.

This second funeral was much the same as the other in Penticton with all the singing and talking and praying. I didn't think I could cry anymore but there you go; it turns out your tear ducts stand by you as long as you need them. Pero Gojević, born October 19, 1918 in Dubrovnik, Yugoslavia, was buried in a quiet graveyard in a Vancouver suburb. It was a clear, windy day in spring in a part of the cemetery that was backed by a row of tall trees. There were vast open spaces then. Now when I go to visit I have to be careful not to walk on a grave. Poor Dad—no privacy, no peace, crowded even in death.

We had a social after the funeral, and this one was at least made more palatable with booze. The O.W. wasn't around so Mom reverted to the wife. She was consoled and fussed over and she took it all with surprising grace and great good form. We all thought she would get drunk right along with us but she didn't. Mom always liked occasions, and this was certainly an occasion. She saw the rich drama available and her important role in it and played it for all it was worth, and she did it with a dry eye.

The rest of us drank and cried and drank some more. Then the brothers and sisters went out into the backyard of Mom's rented fourplex to have our pictures taken. There we are smiling away, as if we were at any other party, as if it were just another opportunity for us to get together and have a few drinks. The wind was blowing so girls' skirts and guys' ties are flipping up, festive and happy. We consoled ourselves by saying Dad would have appreciated the party mood.

∼

*Adrian O'Connell, Family Friend, Kathleen O'Connell,
Kevin O'Connell, Eileen O'Connell*

It's a Long Way to Tipperary

And now we return to Paso Robles, California. Do you remember that Bulgarian movie director, master of the film noir? Well, he hadn't just been sitting around drinking vodka all this time. No, indeed; he had been planning and plotting, and this time he decided it was Mom who was far too happy. What was needed this time was some gut-wrenching sadness. Cue the subdued lighting and the sound of cellos. Bob died. Mom nursed him through what turned out to be a mercifully short passing. And that was that. He was gone and Mom was alone again. Her little bit of heaven had lasted three years.

Now what was she to do? She liked California, the sun, the daily round of ladies' visits and hairdressers, the unfamiliar friendliness of the Americans and the dry cleanness everywhere, but without Bob there wasn't any reason to stay.

Bob's children thanked Mom for her dutiful care but certainly didn't beg her to stay. They were always a little in awe of her. She'd had twelve children and she seemed so foreign with her accent and culturally different ways. They probably should have resented her stepping in like some over-the-hill femme fatale, but they probably were happy Bob was happy, and he hadn't left them out in the cold either.

I met most of them once on a trip to Paso Robles. They seemed harmless enough, a lot like I thought most Americans were like—big, happy kids with twisted pasts. In fact, Bob's son had been in Vietnam and hadn't fared too well as a result. He needed special care,

Mom said. I liked Bob's family; they were just slightly off centre and seemingly non-judgmental, a rarity in my circle.

Mom eventually drifted home and began to be the kind of person no one really knew. She became a bit of a gypsy. This was startling considering that other than the forced march from our burned house and the move from our starter home on William Street she had been content to stay in one place for a very long time. Now with amazing ease she was moving around the city, first living alone, then living upstairs from Tony and Arlene, then in the basement suite of Brendan and his wife, Pam, and then in the nanny suite of my sister Eileen and her husband, Barrie.

In these arrangements there was a common thread. Mom had become a really annoying person to live near. If she wasn't sleeping, burning pork chops, doing the "Scramble" in the paper or drinking endless cups of undrinkable coffee she was complaining. Like a young child she wanted her independence but she still wanted to be attended to, fussed over and treated like a queen. The only way to avoid her wrath was to attempt to anticipate her needs like a really good butler or lady in waiting. Sometimes you got it right and there would be peace. But if you missed the mark by not being there often enough, or too much, or asking too many questions or wearing the wrong thing—"You know, Pauline, your neck is too short to wear that kind of sweater"—or daring to ask what she had done that day, then watch out. Mom was like good wine gone to vinegar. All the things that had made her a vibrant, interesting, vital woman were still there but turned sour. She demanded time and attention more and more each day, like a bottle you just couldn't fill. Simple things she used to do for herself she now thought others should do for her. We all became her unpaid help.

Even though she was the centre of all our lives it really wasn't enough. She wanted—no, she needed—a man to make her feel special again, and so she began a search. This was pre-Internet dating time, so she put an ad in the paper.

To no one's surprise she got many hits. She went to a variety of coffee-shop meetings. She came home with stories of men who were too fat, too stupid, too bald or just plain ridiculous. We found it funny and often laughed about Mom's need for a man until the day she met Bob Number 2. This fellow was short like Bob Number 1 but a little rounder. He had an amazing head of thick, white hair and he was British. In what seemed like the wink of an eye he had moved in with Mom. When we asked what the great attraction was she said, "He brings me tea and cookies in bed. Oh, yes—and when he saw me lying on the bed with just my leg outside the covers he said I looked like Venus." Well, what do you say to that?

He was an old charmer if a bit of a blowhard. He squired Mom around to family gatherings where we took turns listening to his stories. He only had a few and he told them again and again. Still, Mom seemed happy and it meant we were off the hook for a while.

We wanted it to work and for Mom to be happy again. But if something seems too good to be true... Mom started to talk about how Bob was using her money to invest in all manner of strange inventions. Somehow he had got access to her bank accounts and money was disappearing. It took us a while to realize the depth of the problem, but by then Mom had lost a lot of her savings and he was starting to deplete her chequing account.

During this time Mom and Bob had been living in Eileen's nanny suite. It was decided that Bob had to go. Mom was strangely ambivalent about his removal in spite of his bad money behaviour. "Who will bring me tea in bed?" she said.

But a plan was made, and with no warning to Bob the men of the family moved in and he was moved out. That was the end of Mom's foray into the dating scene. It left her with less money but no less interest in men. She continued to say how much she would like to have a man around the house again. We were not very supportive of this idea after what Bob Number 2 had done.

(We heard later that Bob had moved back to England where, as a former member of the British army, he received a pension. He had been ill although we never knew it. He died on an operating table somewhere in Liverpool. We had known very little of him except the lies he told. A conversation Mom had later with his sister revealed a man who had lived a life of deception and had alienated himself from his family.)

Objects in Mirror Are Closer than They Appear

For a while there was an uneasy peace, then mysterious ailments began to weave a tapestry of complicated medications and timings. These changes were taking place while most of us were trying to live our own rather complicated lives. Mom was on a special track to oblivion; we just didn't realize it yet.

Oh, we heard rumours, mostly from Mary Anne: "You know she says she went grocery shopping but there is nothing in her fridge." Or, "I got a call from Safeway to come and get her. She had started shopping and had been in the store for two hours wandering around. Finally someone noticed her just standing there with a buggy piled high with food and when they asked where she lived she couldn't remember. They found a card in her purse with my number on it."

If you've ever watched a flower unfold using time-lapse photography you know that actually sitting and watching that flower bloom in its natural time would be mind-numbingly boring. The photography is only interesting and compelling because you can see the flower quickly morph from start to finish. Mom's losing her mind was like watching that flower bloom in real time. Instead of becoming something sweet and beautiful, however, she became someone quite unrecognizable. There was a slow devolving into despair. At one point Mary Anne called a family meeting; we needed to talk about "what to do about Mom."

We have always gotten together for a variety of reasons—some fun, some not so fun. There was always talk and food and booze. If you got bored or angry with someone you just walked away to another room and talked to someone else. But this time was different. This time we had to gather in one place and stay there. If you had a video camera recording it you would have seen a gradual movement from a party atmosphere to something very dark and dense.

This meeting was something most families would have never attempted, and for good reason. But we did, and it was loud and aggravating and sometimes foolish. Egos floated high like so many multicoloured balloons. Many methods for getting and keeping attention were used. There were tears, too, but no one appreciated this approach; it was too obvious and too easy to ignore. Shouting is an Olympic sport in our family and each person jockeyed for position, raising their voice and the stakes higher and higher.

At one point Eileen's husband, an old hippie type, brought out his First Nations talking stick. He declared that we needed to use it if we wished to speak. It had a limiting but limited effect.

Everyone spoke, even those, like Brendan, who rarely did. He said he'd wondered if Mom was losing it a long time ago when she lived with him and his wife in their basement. He'd put her crankiness down to just wanting attention and her own way.

There was a feeling among many of us that, yes, that was the problem. Many families know a parent is losing it because suddenly they aren't the parent they always knew. The patient, alert person has become someone who was now impatient and befuddled. But how were we to know Mom was no longer herself when she seemed to be the same demanding, fault-finding woman we had known for the last few years. She was just an extension and exaggeration of the woman she had always been.

Because she was a nurse and lived fairly close to Mom, Mary Anne had become her go-to girl. Mom called her several times a day and Mary Anne went over there every day, sometimes twice. You could argue—Mary Anne certainly did—that we should have known how bad things were, but we didn't. Most of us were not there every day and we didn't call her every day, either. This meeting made it fairly clear that while we were whistling in the wind Mom had been busy losing her mind.

We all felt guilty, but Mary Anne didn't really want that. What she really wanted was us to say the words that would have been a balm to her soul: "You are the best, the most attentive, the most self-sacrificing of all of us and even though you don't really think you are a good person, or worthy, we do." But you know how it is when you know someone wants something. It makes you just not want to give it to them even more. That was what was going on.

Finally, someone—probably Helena—cajoled the words Mary Anne needed to hear from us, but they had to be dragged out of us and didn't have the sweet taste Mary Anne wanted or deserved. She cried. She yelled. She left the room. She was coaxed back in.

Anita has always overestimated the power of self-deprecation as a communication tool, which is surprising since she uses it so often and to such little good effect. Once again she dragged herself backwards through a verbal thorn bush. "I should have known. I was there almost as much as Mary Anne but she just seemed unhappy, and her rudeness and put-downs are just so normal to me."

Mom's cruelties to Anita were a legendary and puzzling part of family history. No one had ever actually heard her say the terrible, almost unbelievably cruel things Anita said she said to her, but we knew she must have said them because Anita carried around the weight of Mom's disdain like lead weights. She reported back when Mom said, "You do know the only reason boys like you is because of your big breasts," and she told us when Mom declared, "Your children are not like the rest of the grandchildren; they are so selfish, just like your husband," and "I really do not like the way you clean up, Anita. You just hide everything in drawers; that is not the way it is done." Mom delivered a long, sad litany of complaints, failings and judgments, some deeply personal, some just so mundane and wearing like water on rock.

If anyone had a right to disavow and refuse to accept any responsibility for the sad state of Mom's mind it was Anita. But she wore it like a big old hair shirt. When we tried to say, "Hey; it's okay; it's not your fault," she deflected our comments. "No, no," she said. "I should have done more, I should have seen what was happening."

I wished she would say something like Mom would have said: "You get what you deserve," or "As you sow so shall ye reap," or "She always did seem a bit off." It would have been such a relief for her, but she couldn't. There were too many years of being the good child and doing the right thing. It's too bad, as I'm sure it would have felt good to her.

Everyone else, meanwhile, decided to try not to be the person the family had decided they were a long time ago. The usually uninterested, detached one became interested and asked insightful questions. "Really," he said. "She's been just sitting in a chair wetting herself, for how long?"

Helena, as usual, tried to organize the affair. This time there was competition for who was in charge, who had the saddest story or the most questions and who visited Mom the most times. Mary Anne and Anita were not about to give up their roles as martyr and supplicant easily. I had been a school administrator for a few years and thought I'd try out my newly acquired organizational skills. My attempts at "summarizing succinctly" were met with deserved derision. I still hadn't internalized what it meant to not rush things along.

This meeting, which we thought was about Mom, turned out to be about us. We were finding out where we were in our lives and the reasons why we didn't "get" Mom. All that angst takes a long time to play itself out, but eventually even this family of talkers ran out of steam.

The shouting died down and somehow we came to the conclusion that: a) Mary Anne had been doing too much on her own —"No, no, it's not that. I just think you should know how bad it has become with Mom." Right.—and b) we all needed to get involved in her care and there needed to be a schedule. This was the time for folks to lobby for position as most dutiful child. It was fruitless, really; some of us had more access/time/opportunity to be with Mom.

In the end each of us was given a night to be with Mom, which meant bringing either the ingredients for dinner or a made dinner, staying with her while she ate, talking or watching TV, then ensuring she took her meds and was in bed before we left for the night.

These Mom vigils were painful in the extreme. The truth is most often we do good things because it makes us feel good. There is payback even if it is not tangible. Looking after Mom in her smelly, cramped apartment had no up side. No matter what you said you were met with anger, derision or confusion. These were not friendly times to chat with her and share a meal. Most of the time was spent enticing her to eat what you had made or brought. It took forever. And then there was the long and painful task of getting her changed, into her nightie, meds administered and her tucked into bed.

It should have been a soothing, helpful thing to do but it wasn't. I think we knew we were just marking time. When I left her after all the steps had been taken care of, locking the door behind me, I always felt a deep malaise. It was a combination of sadness at what was happening to her, anger that I could do nothing about it and fear about where this was going.

Driving over to her apartment in rush-hour traffic for an hour-plus after work gave me lots of time to think about Mom. I've always known I wished I had a different mother. I wanted a kind, sweet mother. I wanted a mother who met you at the door with cookies and didn't berate and criticize. I wanted a mother who wasn't worried about seeming vain and would brag about you to others—only she wouldn't think it was bragging; she would just think that is what mothers do. My Mom would think her kids were the greatest. I wanted the mythological Mom I had read about.

Instead, I got a fiercely proud Mom who made babies like jelly beans, worked harder than she ever wanted to, protected and fed us and just "knew what was right." She gave us everything she could and did everything she could, but none of that included being the mom of my dreams. That was far more my fault than hers. This Mom had her own beliefs about how mothers behave and love their children. They look after them and stand up for them. They sew them Halloween costumes and demand order and obedience. They accept their children's hugs as their due. Above all, they don't go overboard with affection because where does that leave mothers? They will use up their whole store of love and be left empty. They must always and at all times remain the centre of the whirl around you, always the eye at the centre.

She was at her deepest core a great storyteller. She told herself and anyone who would listen great tales of how life should be lived. She created her greatest story—"My Family"—and peopled it with characters she knew intimately; she maintained and polished those characters throughout her life. As her mind lost its way she clung to those bits and pieces she knew to be true.

"You are the hardworking, reliable one." "You are the smart one." "You are the funny one." "You are the bad one." "You are one I don't know." "You are the broken one to be protected."

Mom's dementia robbed her of her stories. All the pieces were there, but so jumbled they were just like those boxes of Bits & Bites snack food. Every time she spoke she reached her hand into her new, changed brain and brought out a handful of memories all jumbled together. Individual pieces were recognizable but the whole was not quite right. The thing she had known so well—her family, her role in that family, all those vital connections, her life—they were drifting away slowly like dandelion heads, just drifting.

We knew our attempts to keep Mom at home through the ongoing vigils, multiple phone calls and mini-crisis management would not, could not, last. Visits to gerontologists confirmed that all was not as it should be. Mom had been having mini-strokes and she was definitely not, as they say, thinking straight. In fact, she had really stopped thinking. She was just being.

I called her one day, just to check in, and she said, "Do you know where I am, dear? I have just moved and I am looking out the window and I really don't recognize anything." She said this in a very bright and calm voice, as if she were asking me if I knew where a pair of shoes she had misplaced might be. It was an advanced version of the way she had been greeting me for quite a while: "Well, hello, dear. How did you find me now that I've moved?" Just below the surface I could hear the terror.

I called the social worker who had been working with us and watching a story unfold she had probably seen so many times. She said that maybe now it was time to consider "another setting" for Mom. Like repositioning a plant for better light. We did move her, and rather quickly it seemed to most of us.

It was a strange time. We were glad Mom would be safe in a place she would be closely monitored and given her medication at the proper time and dosage. It also made us very sad, with a hint of guilt overarching. Here we were, ten of us (Timmy and Peter didn't count), and we couldn't look after our own mother? We had to put her in a home where others, not family, would care for her? What was the matter with us? We all shared this sentiment to some extent. But, ultimately, we also knew we couldn't give her what she needed to be safe.

With the help of a social worker, we found a care facility. It was one of those very big places, like a huge mouse maze with long corridors and many small connecting rooms. There were pictures of the occupants on the doors of their rooms to help them remember, "This is what you look like, and this is where you belong." It was filled with old people moving aimlessly around, up and down and in and out of each other's rooms. They shuffled and smiled and stared at you long and hard.

"Do you know me?" one of them asked me one day. "Sure," I said. That is all she wanted—recognition that she was still there, that she hadn't disappeared. They were mostly she's; the he's had long given up and gone.

Mom shared a room with a strangely alert and angry woman sporting an oxygen tank. She was not pleased with the invasion that was the arrival of Mom. There was a curtain separating them, but it may as well have been transparent. We heard her deep, laboured breaths and she heard us trying to pretend Mom was in the best place possible. Familiar pictures were hung, flowers in vases placed in the few empty spaces, a well-known throw placed on her bed. But there was a suffocating air about the whole place that made you want to run the minute you went in. It was grey and smelled like old gravy and pee.

Mom was too confused to be as scared about that place as we were, but she knew she didn't want to stay and that this couldn't possibly be her home. "What am I doing here?" she asked again and again. "I want to go home," she said, alternating between begging and demanding.

The reality was that this bed was what had become available. Since she was reliant on government-assisted care, she had to take what came. Although Mom had Bob's American pension and her old-age pension as well as some money left from the sale of the house, it was still not enough to make a private care centre a possibility. At three to four thousand dollars a month, they were definitely out of Mom's price range. We tried to forget that brief venture into a relationship Mom had taken with the second Bob, that old crook who had managed to take a great deal of her savings to use in his crazy money-making schemes.

When a new setting became available, one that was much preferred by everyone, there was a general sigh of relief. We hadn't seen this place before and were glad it was definitely a step up. This place did have lots in common with her last "home"—it was big, it smelled and it was full of very old, very confused people. It was different in that she had the loveliest room of her own with a big, bay window that looked out onto the garden. She had her own washroom and room for a rocking chair and music.

While the remnants of her life in pictures were once again put up—all the kids, grandkids and great grandkids—it was the pictures of her parents and her and her siblings when they were children that were her talismans. She wanted to look at them and talk about them. They were so real to her, these old black-and-whites, so much more than this strange place. They showed an angelic child surrounded by brothers and sisters you would have identified as little Irish kids just by looking at them.

Here's Mom and her sister Eileen, whom she named her daughter after, wearing dresses with pinafores and the boys dressed in short pants, jackets and knee-high socks. The boys' curly hair is parted unnaturally far off to the side and brushed over in a way that made it look like it would spring free at any moment. These were the pictures she gravitated to and had so much to say about. There was her mother, Helena, after whom she named her eldest child, wearing a severe suit and a rather manly hat with a feather, and her misshapen lip. Mom used to call it her mother's harelip. I never understood how a deep crack in your lip had anything to do with rabbits. There was also a painting of her mother that had been done by one of the women whose houses she cleaned. The painter didn't attempt to cover up the lip but instead spent a great deal of time on her beautiful eyes. They were my mother's eyes.

Helena O'Connell came to Canada for a visit once. I spent a long time staring at that lip. She spoke much the same as Mom but in a strange nasally way I'd never heard before. She seemed very distant and unknowable. She wandered the house day and night, often becoming confused and lost. Mom said it was because she was in unfamiliar surroundings. We didn't know anyone whose mind had lost its way yet, so we accepted her explanation. Grandmother O'Connell didn't stay long, and soon after her return to England she died.

If Mom cried about her mother's passing I don't remember. It certainly wasn't the gut-wrenching display of emotion that erupted in Dad when he got word of his mom's death. She didn't say she missed her or wished she had been with her. She didn't say what a wonderful mother she had been. She may have thought all those things. I imagine she didn't think it proper to indulge in a great display of grief and, anyway, "What good does it do to cry over something you can't change?"

Mom spent a long time looking at that picture of her mother and the one right beside it of her father, James, looking old when he was young. He had chosen a little square moustache above his lip that made him look remarkably like Hitler. I was always a little ashamed of that. What could he have been thinking? Mom had insisted years before that Grandpa O'Connell's moustache had been the height of fashion. Sometimes I would put my finger over the moustache in the picture and then his kind, lost-looking eyes stared straight at you.

Mom's new home had colour-coded hallways and rails along all the walls. These rails were a source of joy to Mom, who recognized them immediately as the rails on all the cruise ships she had ever been on.

"I love this ship; the service is just wonderful." She often asked, "Do you know when we are going ashore? We haven't been in for a very long time and I am sure they are going to run out of food."

Right to the end Mom worried about food. "Look at all these people," she would whisper to me when we went into the dining room that looked very familiar, with all the people sitting at tables being served, and at the same time unfamiliar. "I don't know who they think is making dinner, but it isn't me! I've done my fair share."

We spent a lot of time in that dining room. Mom had always been, next to Tim, the world's slowest eater. Now she took this slowness to an almost Zen-like art form. Each spoonful paused on its way to her mouth and hung there while she became distracted by whatever was in the room.

"What's that?" she'd say, pointing at someone's sweater. "What's that... what's that?" On and on it would go as she tried to name her world. She had a Teflon brain now and all the words just slid off.

She cut her food into tiny, tiny pieces, pierced them with a fork and then moved them around and around her plate. Her napkin became a great source of interest. She'd fold it and fold it, smoothing as she went, and when she had finished with the napkin would begin on the edges of the tablecloth, pulling, smoothing with an intensity in her eyes and an ongoing commitment to this task, all the while a look of self-importance on her face.

"Look at me. Look at me taking care of things, keeping every together. Everything is just fine." Suddenly she would stop and sit very still, her eyes darting back and forth, moving, always moving. She would smile at some poor old soul who would scowl at her. She'd ask them questions, which neither she nor they understood.

She hadn't been in her digs long when she found herself a boyfriend. A man seemed to give her a sense of being, a sense of importance. Even in this state, deep in her brain was the firm belief that a woman without a man was really not worth much. This man was her last conquest. He was a good-looking older man who "read" the paper and talked baseball and nothing much else. Mom didn't care; she didn't even need him to acknowledge her, really; she just liked to sit beside him and hold his hand. "This is my man. I have a man."

This was all well and good until his wife showed up. Younger and aware, she didn't take kindly to Mom's attachment to her husband. The staff soon learned not to have Mom around when she came to visit.

Mom lived in that state of suspended animation for much longer than we thought she would. While she didn't exactly flourish, she was like a plant in a carefully tended garden: not too much of this or that and she was maintained. She was in a special section of the home for the "memory-impaired." It had locking doors that you needed a code to enter and exit. Many of the residents hung around that door, believing this would be the way back to the person they used to be.

In the early days Mom had made her escape. She was long gone before they realized it. Off she went with her walker, walking up and down streets she thought she knew. She finally tired and sat down on someone's front porch. When they asked her, she didn't know her name. It was obviously terrifying, and that was her only bid for freedom.

Many of the others would sit innocently in an armchair in the lounge, looking as if they were just resting, sometimes smiling. At the sight of someone near the door they would tense up almost imperceptibly, then at the last moment jump up and make a mad dash for the door or launch themselves forward with their walkers. You needed to be quick to prevent breakouts. I felt cruel to be the jailer and disappointed that my mom was too far down her memory lane to be one of those who would still try.

Mom's care home floor was called Maple Lane, which sounds all fresh and outdoorsy and suggests vital folks strolling down country byways taking their daily constitutional. To reinforce that image, there were murals depicting winding, woody walkways. There were people walking up and down and up and down those hallways with grim determination to keep moving. Some talked, all the while looking at the floor, not glancing up as you passed by. Some cried while they walked and whispered. One old fellow in particular had a thing for hats and would wear toques, berets, cowboy hats and captain's hats. He completed his outfits with pants hiked up to his armpits and held up with suspenders.

All the women wore some variation on the same theme: a sweater with stretchy waistband pants and comfortable shoes. Mom usually had a scarf and earrings completing her ensemble. That is, if they were in her room. These old gals were notoriously light-fingered and would take jewellery, gifts, cards and the stuffed animals off beds without a thought as they went "shopping" in each other's rooms. It was ironic to feel the freedom to do just as you will just as you lose your will to choose.

These were surreal days for all of us as we watched Mom's gradual undoing. She still smiled when you came to see her, she still talked, but it was mostly nonsense with many unconnected phrases and words strung together in an impossible-to-understand mishmash of ideas. Finally, her body met her mind and there was a united moving toward to the end.

There was no sudden leaving for Mom; she was not to be rushed to her death. Her final gift to us was the time she took to die. She seemed so unbelievably small and weightless, barely making a dent in the bed. Like a small bird with whistling hollow bones, she lay so still and very slowly did the hard work of dying. We sat with her and held her so-soft hands. We brushed her wispy hair and wiped her incredibly smooth skin. We sang to her, a little girl again, and told her stories.

The numbers in the room swelled and receded with the time of day and night. It was never noisy but there was always a hum and always the white noise of Mom's breathing. At one point the priest arrived to administer the last rights. We said the old prayers I thought I had forgotten. We prayed and cried as he said the words of forgiveness and salvation for a soul. Mom would certainly have wanted all that anointing and signs of the cross to see her out in grand style. She would have felt it her due even if she didn't really think she had anything to be forgiven. For most of her life she had done the church's bidding. She had all those babies, ate all that fish and did her duty for as long as she could. Still, if the adherence to the precepts of the church brought her any solace and comfort, we never heard about it.

We are nothing if not a family of drama junkies, so somehow we thought that once she had received the sacrament there would be a flash of light and a burst of angels singing and she would depart. Instead Mom continued on at her own pace. "The girls," as we call ourselves, stayed and stayed. We decided to be with her for as long as it took.

Often throughout her last night her breathing would stop. We would all tense and look at each other. "Is that it? Has she gone?" We stood very still near her bed, we bent our heads low to watch her motionless face, looking for signs of life. Then, with a huge intake of breath, she would begin again. These false stops were like jolts of electricity that left us jittery and slightly hysterical. We told bad jokes, recounted mean and good things Mom had done and then often fell silent with all the things we wanted to say and didn't have the words for.

In the early morning we decided it was time to take a break and went for a short walk in the grounds around the home. For the first time in the days since we had gathered, we were leaving Mom alone. We were surprised to see the world quietly moving along outside her room as if nothing were happening—as if our mother weren't dying just a few steps away, as if it didn't matter, one old woman more or less. The big empty space of outside was more unsettling than being in a room with her dying. We went back inside and settled down to wait. Very soon her breathing stopped again and we stood very still waiting. Then she sighed deeply and died.

I know there is a soul because as she took that last breath and let it go, her very still body changed. It sank into itself, leaving nothing. It wasn't just the lack of breath; there was the lack of her. We held hands and said a spontaneous "Hail Mary," just as if we were believers. Then we cried and kissed her still-warm cheeks.

"Goodbye, Mommy," we all said over and over again. "Goodbye, sweet Mommy."

She was so very human and petty and everyday. She had a power to her that wasn't easily categorized. She could be so good and sometimes so very wrong. She was definitely not boring. She had twelve children—whether by choice or fate or default, it doesn't matter. In the end she left something behind: all those stories. She would have wanted that. She loved a good story, especially if it involved her.

∼

L-R Back Row: Pauline, Mike, John, Peter, Mom, Anita, Mary Anne
L- R Front Row: Tony, Kathleen, Helena, Eileen, Timothy

Afterword

There is a final chapter at the end of a story that often serves to reveal the fates of characters; they call it "The Epilogue." That would be where the answers to pressing questions would be revealed. For example;

"How is Tim is doing?"

"Has Peter has gone back to jail or did he find Jesus?"

Maybe you feel cheated that you can't read more about Michael.

"Is he carrying an emotional scar from the Tim-gets-run-over incident"?

What about Helena?

"Still organizing the universe?"

And Anita,

"Does she continue to soldier on doing battle with all the things that seem to assail her?"

We won't even go into the fact that there are twelve children in the family and only eight really figure in these stories.

"What about the rest of them?"

I would love to give you more details about of all of that but for a small problem. First and foremost is the fact that my family are not characters in a book, although they sometimes act that way. So really it isn't possible to just "fill in the blanks" of people who are still living their lives. But you know like Little Orphan Annie sang, "Tomorrow, tomorrow there's always tomorrow..."

I know too that an epilogue could feature some scenes that might be only tangentially related to the story. However, if I were going to write more about my family it would definitely be up front, in your face, about my family. There wouldn't be a tangent in sight.

Anyway, I warned you in the sub-title when I called it a memoir. I was looking for flexibility and I didn't intend for these stories to follow the traditional arc of my birth to childhood and old age and all the action in between. Instead I have chosen to give you a glimpse into the lives of a seriously large, immigrant family that was and continues to be just a little "different." I don't use the term in a pejorative way, although others might. It is more a statement of fact. I wanted to give you just a taste of what it was like to grow up in an environment that was simultaneously crazy making, and very, very sane. Maybe you saw your family reflected back, if not in numbers then perhaps in style?

In many ways these are just very ordinary lives I've written about. People carrying on with courage through the mundane and often trying bits and pieces that can wear away at us. It is all well and good to carry on when things are all bright and shiny and there is genius to achieve great things and perhaps to receive praise and adulation. But to work away each day with determination to "make the best of it." Now those are lives worth recording.

So yes I am calling this an Afterword. In this way I can, not that I haven't already, but now with wild impunity, speak directly to you the reader in the true style of the Afterword.

"Trust thyself: every heart vibrates to that iron string….".

Ralph Waldo Emerson could have written this line from his poem "*Self Reliance*" yesterday. Writing as he did back in the 1800's it seems he was a bit ahead of the new-age guru trend. It is only after writing this book that I realized that is what I have been trying to do, to listen closely to "that iron string." There I was thinking I was painting this picture of my family when really I was listening to my heart as I wrote myself into understanding. I am fairly certain that anyone reading this little book had already figured that out. I am often the last to know.

Have you ever gone for a long walk and then suddenly for no reason just stopped and looked behind you? It is almost with wonder that you find yourself, just there. Lost in thought, or life, you just arrived. So here I am. A middle-aged woman looking around and wondering how I got here.

Middle-aged? No one ever believes they will get old. That their body will betray them, that the tight, crisp thoughts won't come. This is just not possible. Except that it is. So we look back and see that young self. We see all the big and small, important and petty events that either washed over us or struck us hard and changed us forever.

It is not that anything will change as a result of this reflection. But that rear-view window glimpse is a tender reminder of where we have been. Whatever we are right now and wherever we are right now is where we are meant to be. No matter that we are at times gripped by a desire, a strange and almost desperate need to "have another go at it" to see all the ways that things could have been different. *"If only..."*

Ten-year olds sometimes like to end a story that really has no ending with the very useful sentence, *"And then I woke up and it was all a dream."* Pretty clever I think. And a tactic that I was tempted to use. But this story thankfully doesn't have to have an "ending," at least not one that I have to tell.

After all this is the work of story telling, an old-fashioned sort of activity that is meant to be entertaining but not definitive. It has been an attempt to pass on, to "remember." That is what I have tried to do, to remember my family and myself. Not to re-invent us. Just to put my arms around those things that happened to them and to me and to honour them; to honour the family that we were and the family that we are.

CPSIA information can be obtained at www.ICGtesting.com
225952LV00001B/6/P